D1384892

The Discoveries

James H. Marsh

The Discoveries

James H. Marsh

Consultant
Edward H. Borins

Collier-Macmillan Canada, Ltd.

Acknowledgments

For permission to use material in this book grateful acknowledgment is made to the following: Houghton Mifflin Company for "The Blind Men and the Elephant" by John Godfrey Saxe, and The Macmillan Company for material reprinted from *Exploration and Discovery* by R. Albion. © Copyright, The Macmillan Company, 1965.

Photographs by kind permission of the following: Cambridge University Press, 49 (from *The Beothuks or Red Indians* by James P. Howley); Canadian Government Travel Bureau, iv, 32, 40, 42, 48; Jonathan Cape, 6 (from *Land Under the Polar Star* by Helge Ingstad); City Art Gallery, Bristol, England, 30; Inventaire des Oeuvres d'Art, Ministère des Affaires culturelles, Québec, 37; National Aeronautics and Space Administration, 15, 47; National Geographic Society, 12 (both photos); Public Archives of Canada, cover, 5, 16, 25, 26, 33, 34, 36, 38; Trustees of the British Museum, 13, 17, 20, 21, 35, 46.

Cover Design and Interior Layout: Philip Balsam
Illustrations: Frank Zsigo
Maps: Gus Fantuz and Frank Zsigo
Library of Congress Catalog Card Number: 73-182943
SBN: 02.970280.1

Collier-Macmillan Canada, Ltd.
1125-B Leslie Street, Don Mills, Ontario
The Macmillan Company, New York

Printed and bound in Canada
1 2 3 4 5   76 75 74 73 72

Chapter 1

Man at the Centre

Living in a world of space travel, television and jet aircraft is exciting, confusing, and dangerous. It is exciting because we are always learning more and more about our world and about the planets beyond. It is confusing because of the tremendous amount of information that bombards us from every direction—books, news programs, newspapers, magazines, teachers, and parents. Often the reports are conflicting; one source tells us one thing and another source something opposite. Lastly, many people tell us we live in a dangerous world for many of man's discoveries, automobiles,

The sea has beckoned man from earliest times. First in crude rafts, later in rowed boats, then in tall sailing ships, men set off to find new lands, to escape, to find adventure or to find wealth. Man has sometimes feared the sea and at other times loved it. In the end, the sea took him to the farthest corners of the earth.

aircraft, new drugs and atomic power, for example, could easily work against man, and not for him.

Every man should remember that, after all, he is the centre. He collects the information. He makes the discoveries. He must make sense and order of his world. Still, it is not as though man is facing problems for the first time. He has been in North America for hundreds of years, in Europe for thousands of years, and on earth perhaps for millions of years. His is a long story of struggle and discovery.

Man passes on his solutions and discoveries to the following generations. What if every generation had to re-invent the wheel, or the plough? Of course, every generation is very different, living in different times, thinking different thoughts, facing different problems. An historian must always be aware of the great variety in the story of man, as well as the great similarities. Often the discoveries of one age mean something quite different in another time. Often the discoverers of one age have no idea whatever what the results of their discoveries will be. Our story of the discovery of North America will clearly show this.

History is a way of thinking about man, but what exactly is the study of history? No one can give a simple, clear answer to this question. In the same way it would be difficult to describe exactly geography, biology, economics, art or sociology because each of these subjects studies man in a different way and as long as men study they will never agree on exactly what each subject covers. Before we go on, here are a few opinions some "experts" have expressed about history. Write in your own words what each of the following writers thinks history is, and what each definition tells you about its author.

An account mostly false, of events unimportant, which are brought about by rulers mostly knaves, and soldiers mostly fools.

What is this writer's view of history? What is his view of man? Often we find that the answers to these two questions are the same. Perhaps you already agree with him.

The next writer says what he thinks history *should* be.

It is the mission of history . . . to establish the truth of this world.

This statement may not be altogether clear, but it brings up an important word—truth. What is truth? Why should history be true?

The next writer has a more down to earth view of history.

The history of the world is the record of a man's quest for his daily bread and butter.

The next writer has a warning about history.

Those who do not learn from history are condemned to relive it.

This is another way of saying, as the Bible says, that "there is no new thing under the sun," and that if we look at today's problems carefully we will see, perhaps, that people in the past have faced the same problems.

A famous philosopher who tried the above approach concluded:

We learn from history that men never learn anything from history.

It would be a sad tale indeed if we learned that we learned nothing, and kept on making the same mistakes.

Even though many of our experts disagree on what history is, there are thousands of historians in the world, thousands of history books and millions of history students. Most of them would probably agree on one thing, It is put this way in one more quote: "History is only a confused heap of facts."

Many students will agree, unfortunately, especially when studying for exams. Is that what history seems to be to you? If the study of history were only a heap of facts, it would be boring indeed. Hopefully, we can say, in our own words: "History *should not be* only a confused heap of facts."

Getting the facts

What is a fact? All of us use the word "fact." What do you think it means? Give some examples of facts.

Speaking of facts, one historian gave as an example, Julius Caesar's crossing of the Rubicon River. Then he asked, why is this a fact? Millions of other people have crossed that little river, but they are not written up in history books. Your entering the classroom this morning may be as much a fact as Caesar's crossing of the Rubicon River, but it will never be written down by an historian. There are everyday facts—millions and millions of them—but only a few "historical" facts. An historian *chooses* his facts by thinking about the past. He thinks Caesar's crossing of the Rubicon is important, or as it is sometimes put, *signficant*.

Workers in each field of study choose the facts they think are significant. A chemist concerns himself with different facts from those of a geographer, or a mathematician. In this way, we ourselves remember some things about our past and forget others. Perhaps we try to forget some things that we would rather not remember. Society, too, might like to forget some things, but we believe that our historians should consider each fact on its *significance*, not on how pleasant or unpleasant it is. Perhaps this is what we mean by *truth*.

Facts about the past are the raw materials of history. Collecting them, getting them right and remembering them are important, but only the first step. Making sense of facts, arranging them into a story, and understanding them are the real tasks of an historian or of a history student. When we read a history book we may not enjoy the facts; we enjoy what the historian has done with them.

The following exercise may help us to understand how an historian builds a story from facts.

Study the following list of words and answer the following questions.

dog	lettuce
granite	mosquito
snake	Jacques Cartier
trout	dolphin
Paul McCartney	diamond
iron	monkey
lizzard	apple
turnips	Pierre Trudeau
sparrow	giraffe
gold	whipped cream
ape	

Questions

1. Make a selection from the above list under the following headings.
   a) living b) animal c) mammal
   d) mineral
2. How might you further classify some of the above headings?

This exercise can give us a slight idea of how an historian works in selecting facts, and how he might come up with a different story depending on what he is looking for. Of course, it is much more difficult for an historian who spends long years sifting through thousands of facts, carefully weighing each one, and constantly working to understand them and to fit them together.

The way an historian picks his facts depends partly on what is available and partly on what he wants to say. We should always ask about our historians, "What is he saying?" Summing up how he used facts, one historian wrote:

Facts are like fish swimming about in a vast and sometimes unreachable ocean; and what the historian will catch will depend partly on chance, but mainly on what part of the ocean he chooses to fish and what bait he uses. Of course he chooses his place and his bait according to the kind of fish he wants to catch.

Each historian sees things in a different way. If one hundred artists drew a picture of a mountain, each from a different angle, no doubt each picture would be very different from the others. But because there is more than one picture, does that mean that there is more than one mountain being drawn? The more views we get by the best artists, the more we will know about that mountain. What does this suggest about our knowledge of the past?

The Blind Men and the Elephant

It was six men of Indostan,
To learning much inclined,

Who went to see the Elephant
  (Though all of them were blind),
That each by observation
  Might satisfy his mind.

The *First* approached the Elephant,
  And happening to fall
Against his broad and sturdy side,
  At once began to bawl:
"God bless me, but the Elephant
  Is very like a wall!"

The *Second*, feeling of the tusk,
  Cried, "Ho! what have we here
So very round and smooth and sharp?
  To me 'tis mighty clear
This wonder of an Elephant
  Is very like a spear!"

The *Third* approached the animal,
  And happening to take
The squirming trunk within his hands,
  Thus boldly up and spake:
"I see," quote he, "the Elephant
  Is very like a snake!"

The *Fourth* stretched out an eager hand,
  And felt about the knee.
"What most this wondrous beast is like
  Is might plain," quoth he;
"Tis clear enough the Elephant
  Is very like a tree!"

The *Fifth*, who chanced to touch the ear,
  Said: "E'en the blindest man
Can tell what this resembles most;
  Deny the fact who can,
This marvel of an Elephant
  Is very like a fan!"

The *Sixth* no sooner had begun
  About the beast to grope,
Then, seizing on the swinging tail
  That fell within his scope,
'I see," quote he, "the Elephant
  Is very like a rope!"

And so these men of Indostan
  Disputed loud and long,
Each in his own opinion
  Exceeding stiff and strong,
Though each was partly in the right,
  And all were in the wrong!
            John G. Saxe.

Past is past

The second thing that makes history different from other studies—other than the facts it uses—is its concern with the past. Historians do not believe "what's done is done and best forgotten," although they know that the past is past and can never be re-lived. We can only "go back," not as a traveller "goes back" home, but in our memories. Society's memories are stored in many ways—documents, diaries, newspapers, letters, films, the minds of those alive at the time and so on. These are the only ways we can go back, so we can never get the complete story.

The word "history" itself helps explain what the subject is all about. It is a "story." It usually is about the past. It starts somewhere ("once upon a time"), goes through changes and adventures and on to somewhere ("they lived happily ever after"). The study of history tries to tell us how things *were* and how they *changed*. Once we have these descriptions we ask the age-old questions of how and why? How did it happen? Why did it happen? First, we need the facts.

About this book

A short little history book can barely begin to tell a full story, especially about such an exciting era as the Discoveries. All a little book like this tries to do is to *introduce* the reader to a small part of the story. Perhaps you will find it interesting enough to want to learn more. Our libraries are full of interesting books on the happenings we describe here.

Unfortunately, historians have only managed to dig up a few facts about some parts of this story. It starts when no one lived in the vast northern land we now call Canada. It tells of the first people who crossed from Asia and spread throughout the Americas. It tells of the first ships that made their way to our eastern shores, then disappeared. It tells of the men we now call heroes, who opened up the gates for our ancestors from Europe. These men lived the spirit of discovery. They blazed the way, though they never dreamed of the changes they had begun. In a way, we still live in the spirit of that age, pushing our frontiers into outer space.

Chapter 2

The First Discovery of America

Other fields of study besides history are interested in time and change. Geologists, for instance, are interested in the changes that take place on the surface of the Earth over millions of years. They tell us that before man came to America, about 40,000 years ago, Canada was almost all covered in ice. It is hard to imagine that in the places where today the cities of Toronto and Montreal stand, there was over 1000 feet of ice. However, geologists tell us this is true.

Far to the northwest, though, was a warmer land, free of ice, which we now call Alaska. The geologists also tell us that there was a wedge of ice-free land from Alaska cutting into the continent. Here, about 30,000 years ago, we believe that man made his first entry into North America. The small bands of hunters were probably following game and had no idea they were in a "New World." Every distant place was new to them. They had no reason, or any means, to record their lives. In their very different world, the story of man was "the record of a man's quest for his daily bread." It is even wrong to call it a "record" for these men left no record. They did not write at all. Why do we believe this? Most of us know the countries from which our forefathers came to Canada: France, England, Scotland, the Ukraine, Italy and so on. But where did the Canadian Indian come from? He was here before any of our forefathers. There were many guesses. Some thought they had arrived just before our forefathers did; others that they were survivors of the mysterious island of Atlantis, which had disappeared beneath the sea; still others that they had come from Polynesia far away in the Pacific. Since there were no written records, historians left the puzzle to others. The main detectives were archeologists, men who search out the hidden records of man from what he has left behind. In 1948, Dr. J. L. Giddings found a collection of man-made flints on the coast of Alaska. Scientists told him that they were 9,000 years old. In 1954, Dr. MacNeish of the National Museum found evidence of human life going back 10,000 years. His discovery was made on the Arctic coast. Through finds like these we are piecing together the story of man's first discovery of America, and it goes something like this.

About 30,000 years ago, a small band of olive-skinned people, strong, and probably handsome with straight black hair and dark brown eyes, crossed a strip of land from Siberia to Alaska in search of game. They were not ugly "ape-men" but smooth-skinned, intelligent people, who led an incredibly more difficult life than we do today. They had no guns, no horses, or even bows and arrows. They hunted by spear, and it is the tips of these spears that are the real evidence of man's first discovery of America.

Hundreds and then thousands of these people followed the first few. They came in small bands, and after the ice melted, they spread, over a long period of time, across Canada, the Arctic, the United States and down into present-day Mexico and South America. The descendents of these people have hunted the eastern forests for 6,000 years and there is evidence that they have farmed Mexican soil for 6,000 years, longer than man has farmed anywhere else.

This is one of the greatest stories that we know of man. The accomplishments of these people were very great. Some of them simply gathered food, some hunted, others farmed and some even built great cities. Their story is told in *The Changing People*, another book in this series. If you have already read that book you will know that the story of these people is no longer as happy as it once was. For all their accomplishments they did not have the

power to resist later discoverers, or change sufficiently to compete with them.

In future we will know much, much more of these people and their first entry into America. Over the years you will probably read of new discoveries that will help to piece the story together. Perhaps you will decide to make studies of them yourself. Still, we will never know as much about them as we would like. We know of no "heroes" among these small bands of hunters. History books do not record their names, but they can rightly be called the first discoverers of America.

The Indians were the first discoverers of North America arriving thousands of years before Europeans. The first hunters arrived in Alaska about 30,000 years ago. By the time the Europeans came, these people had spread throughout the Americas and had developed many different ways of life. No previous changes, however, would compare to those that happened after the Europeans came. Often these changes were disastrous, but in the early days many Indians benefited from meeting the Europeans. The Micmac Indians were among the first to meet the explorers and this family shows some of the changes that took place. The Indian enjoyed a way of life that the European never really understood, and he changed it forever.

Chapter 3

The Vikings in America

Canada is a northern land. It shares the top of the globe with Alaska, Siberia, Norway, Ireland, and Greenland, the last great stepping stone across the North Atlantic from Europe to Canada. Greenland, except for a few narrow strips of grass along the southern coasts, is a land of ice. Who called it "green," and why?

Long ago, the people of Norway farmed the coasts around the finger-like fiords, or "viks," of their land, much as they do today. In the winter there was little to do and people gathered around the fireplace and told stories. These stories were told so often that many people memorized every word. In later years, these tales were written down and have come down to us as "the sagas." They told of the feats of those who left the "viks" to seek adventure and fortune —the Vikings. There were many tales to tell, for these fearless wanderers had roamed the world from Russia to

The great Viking sagas were passed on from generation to generation by word of mouth. Later they were written down in the form in which we read them today. They are valuable but confusing documents. This is a photograph of part of the saga about Erik the Red.

Iceland, trading and conquering. They were the most feared warriors, most successful traders and the boldest sailors of their day.

One saga tells of a hot-tempered Viking called Erik the Red, who, after being banished first from Norway and

The Sagas

The Vikings did not leave a written history. They told the story of their deeds to their friends and relatives who passed it on from generation to generation. Many fascinating tales must have been lost, but fortunately two tales of Vinland were later written down. These are the *sagas* and they were not meant to be scientific or geographic. They were told for enjoyment, to amuse and to leave a family record. One is called *The Saga of Erik the Red*, and the other *The Tale of the Greenlanders.*

Until recently the sagas were all the evidence historians had to go on. Sometimes they would believe one saga, then the other, or neither. One saga tells us that Thorvald was killed by a native arrow; the other that he set sail on a later voyage. No wonder the historians had so many different ideas. How much can we believe?

then from Iceland, sailed west into the unknown. He found a new land and as the sagas tell us,

. . . called the land Greenland, for he said that men would desire to visit it if he gave the land a good name.

As it turned out there was some green in Greenland, and Erik did convince several hundred settlers to bring their sheep, cattle, chickens, geese, dogs and children to live there.

Viking ships

In the days when most Europeans were frightened to sail out of sight of land, the Vikings roamed the world. Without even a compass they reached Iceland, Greenland and beyond to the west; Ireland, England, France, and the Mediterranean to the south. They also made overland trips to Russia. The Viking longboat became a frightening sight to seaport towns, and when we picture Vikings today we see them in these long, graceful vessels with the dragon's head on the prow. But for ocean voyages the *knarr* was preferred. It was a broader ship with decks forward and aft. It carried one big sail and oars, and was directed by a steerboard on the right side—hence our word "starboard" meaning right. They were 50 or 60 feet long and fifteen feet wide. (You could step this off in your school hall to get an idea of the size of these vessels.)

The Viking *knarr* was an amazing vessel. Driven by sail and by oars, it was a hardy vessel used for trade, exploration and conquest. The long boards were nailed overlapping each other to give strength on the open sea. For coastal voyages the Vikings used a longer, sleeker vessel called the longship. These were decorated with a dragon's head and shields and became famous all over Europe. The longships were not as stable on the open sea as the knarr.

Viking sailors

Movies, television and books often show the Vikings as huge, hairy creatures wearing buffalo horns and a fur robe. Vikings, to be sure, were fierce warriors, but they were also expert traders, craftsmen and mariners. More likely the explorers who crossed the Atlantic dressed in hooded, woollen gowns. Each sailor had his own leather sleeping bag to keep him warm and dry. They navigated by watching the stars, and the sun, and familiar landmarks. They were bold indeed to sail the vast and often violent North Atlantic.

The little colony took root, and to Erik's credit, lasted almost 500 years.

Two main settlements were established. Brattahlid, the "Eastern Settlement" was on Eriksfiord. The "Western Settlement" was near present-day Godthaab. The hardy Greenlanders set up house, farmed, raised horses, sheep and cattle, and collected wild berries. The men hunted the walrus for his ivory tusks, and captured white falcons to sell to the royal sportsmen of Europe. The women spun and wove wool. In the winter the Greenlanders kept busy carving ivory chessmen, and telling stories around their warm fireplaces. One of the tales they told in later years was of Bjarni, who set off from Norway to visit his father in Greenland. The story as it has come down to us in *The Greenlander's Saga* goes like this:

Bjarni was the son of an Icelander named Herjulf. In his youth he eagerly took to the sea and became a prosperous trader. It was his custom to sail abroad one year and to return the next, in order to spend every other winter with his father in Iceland.

One year Bjarni arrived in Iceland to visit his father but was surprised to learn that he had set out with Erik to Greenland.

"What will you do now?" his crew asked.

"I will take the ship to Greenland if you will go with me."

They all answered that they would follow Bjarni, wherever he decided to go.

Then Bjarni said: "Our voyage will seem foolish since none of us have ever been there before."

So Bjarni and his crew put to sea. In three days they lost sight of land. Then the fair wind failed and changed into north winds and fog. They had no idea in which direction they were sailing and went on like this for many days.

When the sun came forth again, they got their bearings, hoisted sail and sailed for a day before they sighted land. They wondered what land it could be. Then Bjarni said he did not believe it to be Greenland. As they sailed closer they saw that the land was mountainless. Its low hills were wooded.

They sailed two more days before they sighted another land. When they drew near they saw this land was flat and thickly wooded. Bjarni had been told that in Greenland there were mountains and large glaciers and so he knew that this land was no more like Greenland than the first.

Once again the wind failed. The crew wanted to land and take on wood and water. Bjarni refused, telling them: "You have no lack of either."

They hoisted sail again and sailed out into the high seas, with gales from the southwest, and after three days saw a third land which was high and mountainous. Bjarni still did not wish to land, so they sailed along the coast and saw that it was an island.

Then the wind rose mightily and they sailed for four days. Then they saw a fourth land, and this time Bjarni said: "This is most like Greenland."

Bjarni was right. As it turned out, he had dropped anchor in the very harbour where his father had settled. It was a fitting reward after sailing for 3,500 miles. Bjarni showed no further interest in the new land he had seen. Others, however, were more curious. We can take out a map and guess

The European discovery of North America, like so many other great historical events, was largely luck. Bjarni, blown off course sighted what was probably Newfoundland, Labrador and Baffin Island, before finally reaching his destination in Greenland.

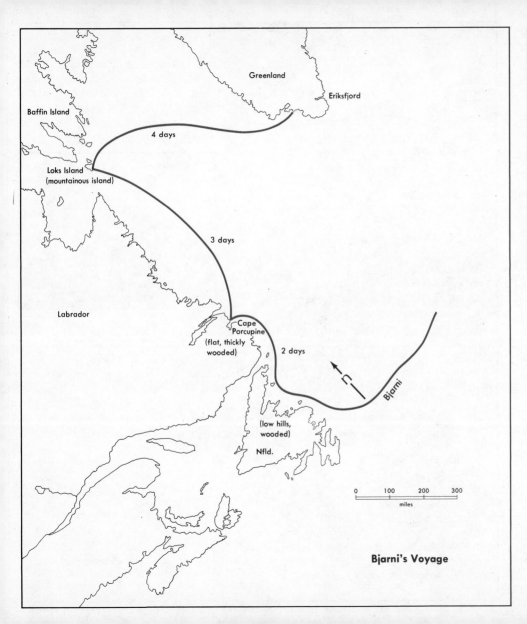

Bjarni's Voyage

Bjarni's voyage

The sagas tell us that Bjarni got lost on his way to Greenland. Where did he go? What new lands did he see? There are many different ideas. Our map shows one likely possibility worked out by Helge Ingstad while sailing up the coast himself. One excerpt of the saga numbers the three places Bjarni saw, while the sailing time, in days, is marked in italics.

Whether or not this guess is right in details, one thing is sure—the first discoverer of America was not Christopher Columbus in 1492, but Bjarni in 986.

where Bjarni had been, but if those in Greenland who talked about the new land wanted to find out more about it, they were going to have to go and see for themselves.

Lief "the Lucky"

Lief Ericson, "Erik's son," a "big, handsome fellow, shrewd and clever, and respected in every way" showed particular interest in Bjarni's discovery. The saga goes on to tell his story:

There was now much talk of voyages of exploration. Lief, the son of Erik the Red, came to see Bjarni and bought his ship and engaged a crew.

Lief asked his father Erik to lead the expedition, but Erik said that he was

9

Lief's voyage

Lief set off in the summer of 1001 and reversed the order of Bjarni's voyage "finding first that land which Bjarni found last." It was stoney and useless and very likely Baffin Island. Next he came upon white beaches and forest. The white beaches are a valuable clue as they are most likely the thirty-mile long beaches on the Labrador coast. If we measure two days sailing, with a good wind from these "Wonder Strands" we find that the next landing was very likely Belle Isle, "an island to the north of the mainland." They then steered between Belle Isle and a cape (probably Cape Bauld) and then westward (left on our map) to their landing place, which they later called Vinland.

too old now and did not have the strength he once had.

Lief and his men prepared their ship, and put out to sea. They came first to that land which Bjarni had sighted last. They cast anchor, lowered a boat and went ashore. The land was rocky and had no grass. They all agreed it was a barren and useless land.

Lief reversed Bjarni's route from Baffin Island to Labrador, to Newfoundland. We are placing Lief, as Dr. Ingstad suggests, at L'Anse au Meadow. We cannot be positive, however, that Dr. Ingstad's site is the right one, but Vikings certainly lived at L'Anse au Meadow, and it is a good guess that it was Lief's party.

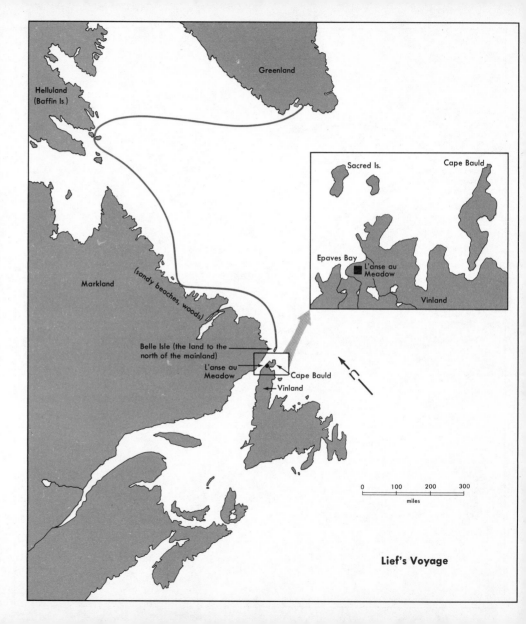

Greenland

Helluland (Baffin Is)

Markland

(sandy beaches, woods)

Belle Isle (the land to the north of the mainland)

L'anse au Meadow

Cape Bauld

Vinland

Sacred Is.

Cape Bauld

Epaves Bay

L'anse au Meadow

Vinland

0   100   200   300
miles

Lief's Voyage

Then Lief said, "At least, unlike Bjarni, we have come ashore on this land. Now I will name this land *Helluland* (meaning 'stone' land)."

They put out to sea and on the morning of the third day sighted a second land covered with forests. Its white and sandy beaches sloped gently to the sea. Then Lief said, "We shall name this land according to its natural resources and call it *Markland* (meaning 'forest' land)." They hurried back to their ship, as a northeast wind was rising.

They then set sail before this northeast wind and were at sea two more days before sighting land. They sailed towards it and cast anchor off an island to the north of the mainland. The weather was fine and the dew lay heavy on the grass.

Lief and his men returned to the ships, left this island and sailed around a cape jutting out from the mainland.

They steered west past the cape and found great shallows at ebb tide, so that their ship was beached and lay some distance from the sea. But they were so eager to go ashore that they could not wait for the tide to rise under their ship. They ran up on the shore to a place where a stream flows out of a lake, where they cast anchor.

Lief sent out his men to inspect the country. They found grassy meadowlands for the cattle, salmon in the rivers and fields rich with wild wheat.

. . . they took their leather sleeping bags ashore and built themselves shelters. Later they decided to stay there during the winter and set up large houses.

Lief's father-in-law, Tyrkir, a German, was late returning from his explorations. "Where have you been?" Lief asked him. Tyrkir grinned and answered "I have found grapes and vines!" Lief could hardly believe him. The next day, though, all agreed that Lief's name for the new land was fitting—*Vinland.* In early spring the men loaded their ship with a cargo of timber and grapes, and set sail for Greenland.

On the trip back, Lief rescued fifteen shipwrecked sailors from a reef. This deed earned him the nickname by which we know him today—Lief "the Lucky."

The Last Vinland Voyages

The sagas tell of three more voyages to Vinland. Thorvald, Lief's brother, was the first European to encounter the native peoples of Vinland, whom the Vikings called *Skraellings.* Unfortunately, it was an unhappy beginning. Thorvald's men set upon nine defenseless natives and killed eight of them. In turn the Skraellings attacked the Vikings, and in the battle Thorvald was killed.

The next voyage was undertaken by a Norwegian trader, Thorfinn Karlsefni,

"a well-bred, well-built and noble man of great wealth." He set out in a serious attempt to colonize Vinland with 250 settlers and a herd of livestock. The first winter was especially severe. The cattle died and the fishing was poor, so Karlsefni decided to move the colony southward along the coast to a little bay they called Hop. A few weeks later the colony had a visit from some Skraellings who were terrified by a bull which "began to bellow and carry on in a frightening manner." They had never seen these creatures before. The sagas describe the scene.

Then the natives were terrified and ran off with their packs which contained all kinds of furs. They ran towards Karlsefni's house and wanted to get inside, but Karlsefni placed guards at the doors. Neither party could understand the other's language. The natives unslung their packs, untied them and offered their wares. They asked for weapons in exchange, but Karlsefni forbade his men to sell weapons. He told the women to carry out milk to them, and as soon as they saw the milk they wanted to buy nothing else. Thus the Skraellings carried away what they bought in their stomachs, leaving Karlsefni and his men with the packs of furs.

It seemed that Vikings and Skraellings might get along after all, but a later meeting led to battle. Karlsefni decided to give up and go home to Greenland.

Where is Vinland?

Our description under "Lief's voyage" seems pretty sensible to sailors, but is it right? Are the sagas accurate enough? They tell us that Tyrkir found grapes, and grapes only grow much further south (see "the grape mystery"). Where was the Vinland campsite? Historians (and others) have offered the following suggestions: Greenland, Labrador, St. Lawrence Valley, Newfoundland, New Brunswick, Nova Scotia, New England, Maine, Boston, Cape Cod, New York, Carolina, Florida (and others). It seemed as if we would never know for certain. Then, in the early 1960's, a Norwegian, named Helge Ingstad, and his wife Anne, located a spot in northern Newfoundland which fits the description in the sagas. Years of digging have uncovered two large houses and several small ones, very like those found in Greenland. They had clay floors, turf walls, timber roofs and a central hall with a fire pit. The Ingstads also found a Viking tool used for weaving and a bronze pin. They, and many historians, are convinced that Lief's colony built this settlement. Behind the site there are salmon streams and a meadow, and seaward there is a shallow bay. There is no doubt that Vikings built this settlement, but was it Lief? Can we know for sure? One historian suggests that the site is too small for Lief's expedition, and that it may have been built by some of those

© National Geographic Society

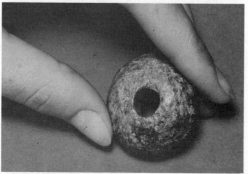

© National Geographic Society

A modern-day Viking explorer, Dr. Helge Ingstad retraced the paths of the Vikings and discovered the ruins of what was probably a Norse settlement dating around A.D. 1000. In the top photo Dr. Ingstad brushes off the remains of a fireplace in a large house, which measured 60 by 45 feet. Nine houses were discovered near L'Anse au Meadow, on the northern tip of Newfoundland. Dr. Ingstad believes that it is possible that Lief Ericson founded the settlement.

Below is a photo of a tiny wheel, part of a spinning device, carved out of soapstone. It is the first Viking household article ever unearthed in North America, and adds important proof that Vikings tried to settle in the New World long before Columbus. Dr. Ingstad's wife, Anne, found the spindle wheel at L'Anse au Meadow.

lost at sea on the way. The future will probably see new theories, and, hopefully, new evidence.

The grape mystery

The sagas tell us that Tyrkir, a German, found "vines and grapes," and thus gave Vinland its name. But the farthest north that grapes grow in America is around Boston, almost 2,000 miles from Greenland. This would have taken at least 14 days to sail. But the sagas tell us that Lief sailed only five days from *Helluland* (Baffin Island). How can we tell which is correct in the sagas—the sailing time of five days, or the finding of grapes? They both cannot be right. Here are a few questions you can ask to help make up your mind.

1. Did Lief call his new land Vinland for the same reason that Erik called his discovery Greenland, that is, to make it sound better?

2. We know that many berries grow in Newfoundland and that Vikings made wine from such berries. Is this what they meant by Vinland?
3. In Viking language Vinland could also mean "land of grass." What might have happened to the account over the years?
4. Lief, the saga tells us, loaded his ships with grapes in the late winter or early spring. When do grapes grow?

The Skraelling mystery

The Vikings were the first Europeans to meet the people of North America. Who were they? Eskimos? Indians? Which tribe? The Vikings called them "small ugly men with coarse hair; they had big eyes and broad cheekbones." How much does this help us?

We are also told that the Skraellings ate blood and marrow. Since we know that the Eskimos and Indians both ate this mixture, the information helps prove that the Vikings met the natives, but does not help as to which. The following clues are a little more helpful.

1. The Skraellings had skin boats large enough for three people to sleep under. Eskimo kayaks are much smaller. Indians often liked to sleep under their canoes.
2. Karlsefni traded the Indians milk for furs—inland furs like marten. The Eskimos are coastal people.

The controversial "Vinland Map" was drawn before Columbus' voyages. Many use it as proof that the Vikings discovered America. Others are not so sure. Who drew it? What areas does it show? How did the map maker know Greenland was an island when this was unknown until this century? There are many mysteries concerning the Vinland map.

The sagas tell us that the final attempt to colonize Vinland was led by Freydis, Lief's half-sister, and two brothers, Helgi and Finnbogi. It ended up a total failure as the party, as though they did not have enough problems, fought among themselves. It was an unhappy ending for the little colony.

Conclusion

Not so long ago people doubted that the Vikings had ever reached America. Today, there are many questions unanswered, but some things are sure: Bjarni was the first European discoverer of America, and Lief was the first European to set foot on the new

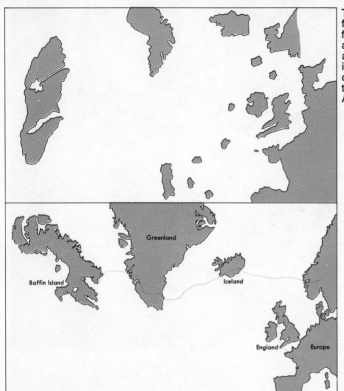

These two maps show the famous Vinland Map drawn before Columbus' voyages, and a modern map of the same area. Match up the same areas in each map. Why would some consider this map to be proof that the Vikings visited North America?

Greenland

Baffin Island

Iceland

England   Europe

land, and to try and set up a colony.

On the one hand, the story of the Vikings in America is a romantic tale of bold explorers. On the other hand, it ends sadly. Vinland disappeared after only a few short years, perhaps from fear of the Skraellings. The Greenland colony mysteriously disappeared around 1400. Europeans almost completely forgot that Greenland ever existed. And they probably never heard of Vinland. The story of the Vikings in America seems one of history's dead ends. It led to no permanent settlement, and Columbus knew nothing of Vinland. Later explorers were not looking for ivory, falcons and Skraellings, but for gold, spices and Chinese.

Nevertheless, it all happened. Historians are concerned with piecing together the facts as best they can. It is for the rest of us to use our imaginations to fill in the gaps. Imagine what Canada would be like today if the Viking's colony in Vinland had grown. Who would today's Canadians be?

Things to do:

For those who are interested in the Vikings and their adventures, there are some fine books in almost every library. Inexpensive, easily read, paperback copies of the sagas are available. *Westward to Vinland*, tells the story of the Ingstads and their discoveries.

Most hobby shops carry a model of a Viking ship which you might find interesting to put together. These models are usually of the Viking "longboat" however, not the *knarr* which we have described.

Chapter 4

Man the Explorer

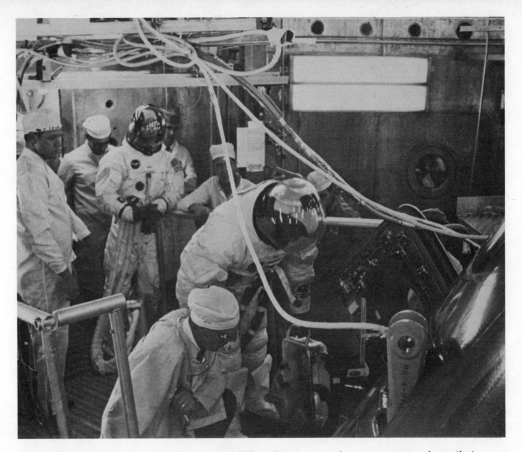

Today offers probably more exciting possibilities than any previous age; so much so that it is hard to keep up with, and understand even a small part of what is happening. Here, modern explorers Russell Schweikart, David Scott and James McDivitt enter their space craft, Apollo 9.

On Monday, July 20, 1969, you probably watched, along with millions of others around the world, as Neil Armstrong hopped down the ladder of his service module onto the surface of the moon. "That's one small step for a man, one giant leap for mankind," Armstrong said. Many felt that this was man's greatest moment ever. This wonderful adventure forced us to change all our ideas about speed, distance, and travel. A hundred years earlier, 60 miles an hour was thought to be about the fastest speed that man could travel and live. The moon capsule, riding on top of a Saturn rocket in 1969 reached a speed of 25,000 miles an hour. In 1869 the trek to the West of North America was a great and dangerous journey taking months of weary travel. The astronauts covered approximately 500,000 miles in just a little over eight days.

Now, if we could take a long journey, back in time rather than into space, we would eventually come to the time when North America was inhabited only by Indians. We would see no highways, no cities, no airports. In fact, our ancestors in Europe were not even aware that this huge land existed! Behaim's Globe (shown on page 16) shows what Europeans thought of their world in 1492.

Behaim's globe was drawn in 1492, before the great explorations. Just off the coast of Africa, the Canaries are shown accurately but between them and "India" the lands and islands shown are just fancy—for instance the fabled islands of Antibia, Saint Brendan, and Brazil. Where might Behaim get his information about Cipango, Java and India? What does the map tell us about the old story that everyone in Columbus' time thought the earth was flat?

Questions
1. What shape did Behaim picture the world as having?
2. Find a map of the world as we know it today. (Your classroom globe will do.) Find Europe on both. What would "Hispania" be? Find two groups of islands on both maps, one just off Europe, the other just off Africa. Name them.
3. What body of land was named in the far East (to the left of the map) Look up "Cathay" in an encyclopedia or dictionary. What large land area was completely missing from Behaim's globe? From where might Behaim have gotten the idea to draw in islands like "Cipango"?
4. What had happened to the knowledge of the Viking exploits over the years? Why might this have happened?

When we see how man has spread across the world and how much he has learned about his world since Behaim's time, we can imagine the importance of those first explorers who, like the astronauts, took "one giant leap for mankind." If the Vikings had written a short and forgotten introduction, these men wrote the first chapter of the New World's history. Like the astronauts, they led the way. Why did they come in the first place? What kind of men were the first explorers? How did they come?

A mountain climber, a scientist, an astronaut or even a week-end camper, all might be called "explorers." Each would have different reasons for "exploring," and if we want to know those reasons, we can ask them face to face. We cannot ask those who lived so long ago. Few eye-witness accounts have survived. Few explorers cared much about writing. Few nations said much about their discoveries because they did not want others to know about them. Let us try to put the story together, like a jig-saw puzzle, with many pieces missing.

The unknown world away from home

For a long time Europeans knew little about the rest of the world. There were no televisions, newspapers, magazines or textbooks. Usually, ships hugged the shores, and their rare trips to distant lands took years. Spices and other valuable goods found their way to Europe from the mysterious East, but little was known of these countries. Life in those days was often short and never easy—even at home. To travel abroad took a great deal of courage.

Marco Polo

Marco Polo was the first European to visit and describe the far East, or "Cathay" as it was known. He was a merchant from the city of Venice, a very rich trading centre. Look up Venice in a textbook or encyclopedia for it is a beautiful city with an interesting history. Marco Polo lived in Cathay for several years around 1290, about 300 years after the Vikings visited Vinland. The following description is from his writings.

. . .The noble and handsome city of Zai-Tun is a city in Cathay loaded with merchandize that is afterwards dis-

Marco Polo is shown here as an older man who has seen much in his life. In fact, Marco Polo did see more than any man of his or any previous time. He was one of history's greatest travellers, and his accounts fascinated readers then, as they still do. His descriptions of Cathay, Cipango and the Indies sparked men's imaginations in Europe. When they finally set sail across the oceans, it was to find the lands that Marco Polo described.

tributed through every part of the province of Mangi. The quantity of pepper imported there is so considerable, that what is carried to Alexandria, to supply the demand of the western parts of the world, is trifling in comparison. It is indeed impossible to convey an idea of the throng of merchants and the mass of goods . . .

Zipangu is an island in the eastern ocean . . . It has gold in the greatest abundance. [Describing the king's palace] . . . The roof is covered with a plating of gold, in the same manner as we cover houses, or more properly churches, with lead. The ceilings of the halls are of the same precious metal; many of the apartments have small tables of pure gold; and the windows also have golden ornaments. So vast, indeed, are the riches of the palace, that it is impossible to convey an idea of them. In this island then are pearls also . . .

An island of very great size, named Java . . . abounds with rich commodities. Pepper, nutmeg, spikenard, galangal, cubebs, cloves, and all the other valuable spices and drugs . . . The quantity of gold collected there exceeds all calculation and belief.

Questions

1. How does Marco Polo describe the city of Zai-tun? What valuable product was traded there?
2. Look back to Behaim's globe. Find Zipangu. From whom did Behaim probably get his information? What present-day island is Zipangu? What riches did Marco Polo find there?
3. Locate Java on a modern-day map. What valuable products were found in Java?
4. Many people read Marco Polo's accounts. His was one of the first books to be printed on the newly invented printing press. In fact, it

was a "bestseller." What would readers think of those lands? Why might Europeans want to go there?

Men of all times have felt the lure of riches but few have had the energy or the means to go after them. Even after Marco Polo, few Europeans travelled to Cathay. Measure the distance overland from Venice to Cathay. Can you imagine such a trip without an airplane, railway or car? If you are interested in Marco Polo, you should read about him and how he travelled to Cathay to meet the great Emperor, or "Khan."

It was not that Europeans did not travel; they did. Fishermen from Brittany, occasional merchant fleets, and earlier, Viking adventurers made their way out into the Atlantic. But the ships were small, unhealthy and dangerous. These were not organized voyages of discovery. They were ignored by geographers and aroused little interest.

Why did all this change? Why did Europeans, after about 2,000 years of fearing the unknown seas, set sail by the hundreds?

Europe in 1500

We mentioned before how little Europeans knew or cared to know about the world beyond their borders. This changed greatly in the era known to us as the *Renaissance.* Slowly horizons expanded and man became

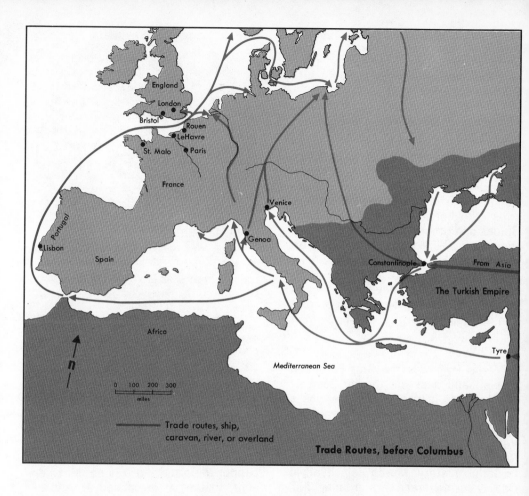

Trade Routes, before Columbus

This map shows Europe in the days before the explorations, when the Indians were the only inhabitants of North America. Not long before, the richest cities were those around the Mediterranean Sea—Venice, Genoa, Constantinople. These cities grew rich by trade with the East from where they bought goods to sell at a profit to the rest of Europe. Then Portugal, Spain, France, the Netherlands and Holland grew in population and their cities grew richer in trade. From the map you can see why these Atlantic countries sought their own routes to the Orient. Prince Henry's ships searched around Africa. Columbus and Cabot searched to the west. One day the Atlantic countries would become very wealthy from their discoveries as they became the centre of trade and of empires.

Questions (Map of Europe in 1500)

1. What parts of Europe in 1500 still have the same names today?
2. Name some present-day European countries not shown on the map.
3. Show the main trade route into Europe. What means of transportation would be used to bring goods into Europe? What two cities received most of the goods?
4. Why would countries like England, Spain, France and the Netherlands be excluded from trade with the Far East? What experience were they getting at sea trade?
5. Locate the Turkish Empire. What would happen if the Turks decided to cut off trade from the East, or to charge huge profits on goods passing through their territory?

---

more and more interested in the world around him. Science and art flowered. Cities grew. Not since the days of Ancient Greece and Rome had man been so active. In fact, the name *Renaissance* means rebirth. It was as if man had been asleep since ancient times and now had awakened. Now man was reaching out across the oceans, and our history was beginning. A study of the *Renaissance* from history books in your library would be interesting and helpful in understanding this era.

Prince Henry the Navigator

Once there was a mysterious land. Somewhere in it there flowed a river of gold. The land was guarded by dragons and fantastic birds. Sheep were as huge as oxen, and giants could wade into the ocean and crush a ship with one hand. Women could slay a man with a glance from their jewelled eyes. A ruler of fabulous wealth named Prester John ruled over this land. Europeans were never allowed there. Today we know this land as Africa.

People often develop strange ideas, even today, about things they have never seen. These wild ideas about Africa could never be tested, so they lived on until the days of Prince Henry, who made the first and most important decision in our story. The following excerpt was written by the historian Henry Hart. It is an example of how an historian chooses certain facts about a man's life and then describes how these facts are important.

The one man to whom more than to any other was due the advancement of nautical science in Europe and the systematic expansion of maritime enterprise in Portugal was the Infante Enriques, better known to the world as Prince Henry the Navigator.

Born in 1394, Henry, the third son of King John I and Philippa of Lancaster, daughter of John of Gaunt, as a boy had heard numberless tales of

the Moors and his people's wars with them. He had heard as well marvelous stories of Africa—of the caravans that came up out of the Sahara heavily laden with ivory and gold dust, ostrich plumes and skins—and lurid accounts of wild beasts and wilder people. From early boyhood he appears to have had his thoughts ever turned to the Dark Continent, of which only the northern fringe was known to Europe. Winning his spurs in 1415 as a soldier at the siege of Ceuta, in Morocco, his experiences there aroused a deeper interest than ever in Africa. He greedily absorbed every available bit of information concerning the routes followed by the caravans from the far interior, and learned much from the merchants of Oran about articles of trade and the people in the hinterland. He added to his store of knowledge the tales of traders from Timbuktu and Gambia and the Niger country. He studied all the maps that he could find—even though they were very crude, and more often inaccurate than correct. He studied minutely the more scientific charts drawn with care by the Jewish cartographers of Majorca. When finally the expedition returned from Ceuta to Portugal, the prince resolved to bend every effort to seek a road to the rich lands of Guinea by way of the sea, and so to avoid dealing with the Arabs of the African Mediterranean littoral. For the remainder of his life (with the exception of certain political episodes with which we are

PRINCE HENRY of PORTUGALL

CEUTA

Prince Henry is pictured as a mighty warrior. He was a successful general but it is for his plans and hopes to have his captains sail to the Indies that he is most remembered. It was he who set up the famous school at Sagres where men could apply science to the problems of sailing at sea. Prince Henry gave the first push that set in motion the Age of Discovery.

the Portuguese coast, he established a school where scholars could study navigation and geography. In a world of superstition and fear, Henry's methods made great advances, and Portuguese sailors became the boldest in the world.

First the Portuguese established bases in the Madeiras, the Canaries and the Azores. Then they progressed down the coast, past Cape Nun and by 1445, Cape Blanco and Cape Verde. To the surprise of some, when the sailors passed the equator, their blood did not boil. An historian of Henry's day listed the following five reasons given by Henry for his decision to go exploring.

i) "a wish to know the land that lay beyond the Canaries and Cape Bojados, and to this he was stirred by his zeal for the service of God and of the King Edward his lord and brother who then reigned."
ii) to develop trade "which traffic would bring great profit to our countrymen."
iii) to learn "how far the power of the infidels extended" in Africa.
iv) to find a Christian King in Africa who would aid the Portuguese in their battles against those infidels.
v) to convert to Christianity "all the souls that should be saved."

Curiosity, Money, Religion. These three reasons occur again and again in our story. Henry's prize was the

not concerned here) he concentrated all his thoughts, efforts, and resources to the accomplishing of this end.

Questions

1. When did Prince Henry first become interested in Africa and the East?
2. What did Prince Henry decide to do? How did he go about this? What studies did he make? Why were these studies important?

3. What did Prince Henry see as the advantage of an African route to Asia? How could he steal some of the trade from Genoa and Venice?
4. What facts about Henry's life did Mr. Hart consider important?

Tall, blonde, muscular, young, courageous and adventuresome, Prince Henry was well cast as one of history's important men. At Sagres, on huge profits now going to Genoa, Venice and the Arabs. As a Christian, Henry would see the spread of his faith. Also, Henry would fulfill his childhood dreams of discovering strange lands.

Prince Henry died in 1460, after 40 years of discovery and study. It was left for two of his countrymen to complete the voyage to Asia. Bartholemew Dias set off in secrecy, followed the coast southward, and after a violent storm found himself around the Cape of Good Hope. But at the very gates of the Indian Ocean, Dias' men, tired and afraid, forced him to return home. Dias supervised the construction of three stout vessels for the final trip to Asia, but it was left to another, Vasco da Gama, to captain the voyage. Da Gama left Lisbon on July 8, 1497 and after many adventures he reached Mozambique, and finally, Calicut in India. When he returned to Lisbon in September 1499, he had been away for over two years and had sailed over 24,000 miles. Only 44 of his original crew of 170 returned alive.

The news that the sea route to Asia had been opened was received with mixed feelings in Europe. What countries would not want a new route opened? What other countries would be interested in the new route? How had man's view of his world changed since 1490 when Behaim drew his map?

VASCO DE GAMA

Vasco da Gama was one of the great captains of the age of discovery. It was he who finally brought the Portuguese flag around Africa and achieved Prince Henry's dream of reaching the Indies. One writer claims that Da Gama, because he carried out orders rather than carrying out his own dream, was more like today's astronauts than Columbus who was a great dreamer as well as a man of action. This portrait shows the explorer in full armour.

21

Chapter 5

The Tools of the Explorers

Prince Henry's enthusiasm spurred the Portuguese in their explorations, but that is not the whole story. A man may dream, but many things must help to make his dreams come true. Henry needed the courage of his captains and the skills of his scientists and shipbuilders. When Henry was young ships were clumsy and slow and navigators had no way of finding their way at sea. If a ship strayed from sight of the coast, it usually was lost. Geographers had great theories about the earth and astronomers great theories about the heavens, but neither one were of any use to the sailor. One or two schools in Europe tried to help the navigator by drawing charts showing coasts, rivers and harbours. Prince Henry's greatest accomplishment was to bring the thinkers together with the doers. The geographers and astronomers would develop the art of navigation —getting around at sea. The ship-

The *caravel* was the type of ship developed by the Portuguese for ocean travel. It combined certain European improvements with the triangular sails borrowed from the Arabs—a good example of how people learn from each other. These ships were small, but were easily handled and sturdy. They carried the Portuguese all the way to India.

builders would build better ships and sailors would learn to handle them with skill.

Finally Prince Henry's work paid off. Many different men combined their thoughts and their skills to make Henry's dreams come true. In the same way today scientists, mechanics, astronomers, astronauts and many others work together to make the dream of space travel come true.

How do you find your way on the open sea, away from shore? Prince Henry's school discovered a way— follow the North Star which never moves out of its position in the sky. Later the noon-day sun was measured to help find the way. This discovery opened many new and exciting possibilities.

Although they seem crude beside today's gadgets, the instruments of the Age of Discovery were very useful. The compass pointed the direction. The log, simply a piece of wood on a long rope with knots tied on it, gave an idea of speed. The sand hour-glass told the time. Finally, the cross-staff measured the height of the sun above the horizon to tell the position of the ships. The observer held this instrument by his left hand and with his right hand lined up with the sun or star—a difficult task on a tossing ship.

The ships of Prince Henry's boyhood were not suitable for exploring strange and dangerous costs. They had difficulty sailing against the wind or close to shore. Over the years,

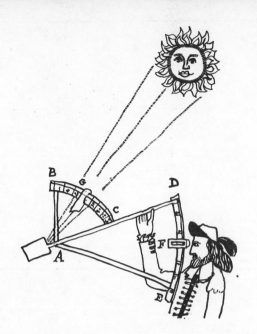

The *quadrant* was a useful instrument developed to measure the altitude of the sun, or North Star, and after some simple calculations, to give your latitude. Knowing your latitude means that you can tell exactly how far north or south of the equator you are.

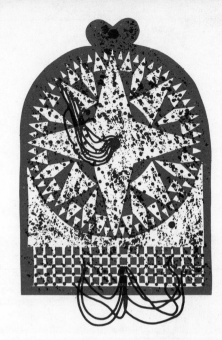

Cabot and Columbus must have had one of these *traverse boards*. This instrument helped the seaman keep track of where his ship was as he zig-zagged, or "tacked," back and forth taking advantage of the wind. The officer of the watch stuck a peg into the board every half-hour for each course the ship sailed. The estimated speed on each course was recorded by the pegs in the bottom holes.

however, the Portuguese developed an excellent little vessel called a *caravel*. As with so many of the great inventions of history, the caravel combined the knowledge of different sources, borrowing here and there. In many ways it copied the Arab ships of the day. The ships of the Age of Discovery were seaworthy, hardy, vessels. They were, however, extremely uncomfortable. They had no sleeping accommodation. The men

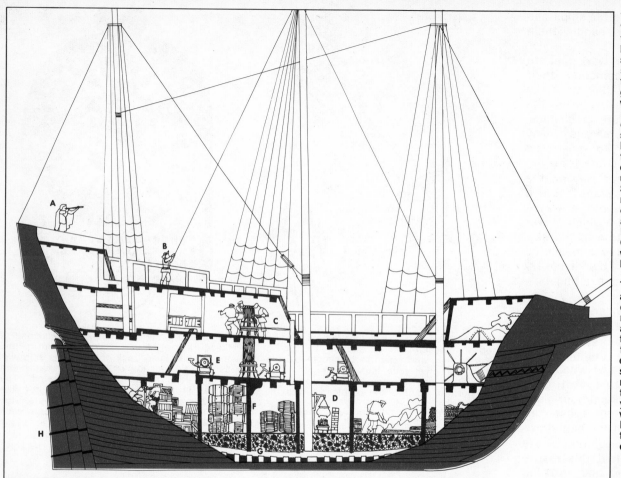

This drawing shows a "cross-section" or inside view of a sailing ship used by the explorers. These ships appear primitive and small to us, but in their time they were one of man's greatest creations. These were the vessels that carried him to the ends of the earth. The letters A to D show some of the tasks to be performed on board, taking directions (A), handling the ropes (B), rolling up anchor (C), cooking (D). Some vessels carried cannons (E), weapons unheard of in faraway lands. Food and water were stored below in barrels (F). The letter G shows the heavy rocks which were used to help keep the ship upright.

To the three masts were attached the sails which caught the wind. Ropes and masts held the sails and adjusted them. It took skill to handle the "rigging", so that the sails could be turned to catch the wind. The ships were steered by the rudder (H). If you are interested in the sailing ship, your library will have books with more information and hobby shops will have plastic models that can be easily assembled.

slept as best they could on deck, bothered by rats and insects. Wet weather soaked everything and the hulls always leaked. The menu was salt beef or pork, beans, peas, and biscuit, with wine.

The changes of history have many causes woven together like wool in a sweater. One cause depends on another and it on still another. One of the reasons that man was able to set out on his conquest of the ocean was

that thinkers and practical men got together and invented ways of finding their position at sea and ships to carry them to the far off places of their dreams.

Chapter 6

A New Heaven and a New Earth

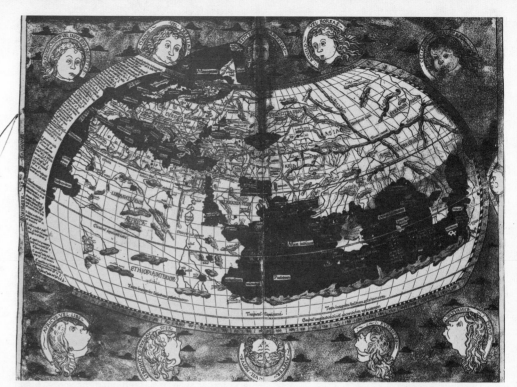

Claudius Ptolemy was the most important geographer of ancient times. He lived about 1300 years before Columbus. He wrote a book describing over 8000 places and drew maps that were respected for over a thousand years. Later, any book on geography was called a Ptolemy, so famous had the geographer become. Still, as you can see from this map, drawn around 1480 from Ptolemy's ideas, Ptolemy was often very inaccurate. What areas were completely unknown? Which areas were highly inaccurate? It is odd that Ptolemy's biggest mistake—making it look like it was only a short distance from Europe across the Atlantic Ocean to Asia—encouraged men like Columbus and Cabot to think they could cross the Atlantic in a short time.

Our map in the last chapter showing Europe around the time of Prince Henry gives us an idea of what Europe looked like and of why different countries became interested in taking to the sea. Compare this map to an atlas map of Europe. Maps can be used to show how things were, as well as how they are today. Trace out the trade routes. Where did the goods come from? Which cities were in the "middle"? How would they profit? Which countries were farther along the routes? Why were they at a disadvantage?

Prince Henry thought that Portugal would profit if he could find a direct route to Guinea. As an historian of Henry's time wrote:

When Prince Henry wanted to obtain information about the more distant parts of the western Ocean to find out whether islands or continents were to be found outside the known world, he sent out caravels to discover these lands.

We saw in Chapter 4 how Henry's captains, and those who sailed for later Portuguese kings, slowly made their way down the African coast. It was a very long and dangerous voyage. An Italian scientist, named Paolo Toscanelli wrote to the Portuguese king and advised him that he was sending his ships in the wrong direction. If he sent them west, Paolo said, they would reach Marco Polo's Cathay in no time. It seemed like an odd idea to sail west to get to the east! King John of Portugal rejected Paolo's suggestion. When another Italian, a Genoese by the name of Christopher Columbus, came to King John with the same idea, the King thought him to be "a big talker, and boastful in setting forth his accomplishments, and full of fancy and imagination with his Isle Cipangu." No, the Portuguese would continue to search out Asia via the coast of Africa. The Italian's plan was rejected.

The Admiral of the Open Sea

Was Columbus "full of fancy and imagination"? How did he come to this wild idea of sailing west to the East? His son Fernando, wrote his version of how his father reached this idea:

He (Columbus) obtained information about other journeys and voyages that the Portuguese were making in Africa, and he enjoyed talking to the men who sailed in those regions. . . . one thing led to another and gave life to many thoughts, so that the Admiral, while in Portugal, began to think that, if the Portuguese could sail so far to the south, it should be possible to sail equally far to the west, and that it was logical to find land in that direction.

There are many portraits of Columbus, but none were painted during his lifetime. This portrait shows what one artist thought Columbus looked like. How does it compare with the following description of Columbus? "The Admiral was a well-built man of more than average height. His face was long, with rather high cheek-bones; his person neither fat nor thin. His nose was hooked, his eyes light, his complexion was also light, with a ruddy tinge. In his youth his hair was fair, but it turned white in his thirties."

It wasn't a new idea; Paolo had thought of it years before. But Columbus was more than a dreamer. He was determined to do something about his plans. He listened closely to the sailors' tales. He learned the science of navigation. He went on many voyages. Historians have discovered

geography books which Columbus studied. Like many students he underlined or made notes about what he thought was important. Some of his notes read:

The earth is round and spherical. . . . Each country has its own east. . . .

Between the end of Spain and the beginning of India lies a narrow sea that can be sailed in a few days. . . .

One can sense Columbus' excitement as he studied and his ideas grew. In a copy of Marco Polo's travels, where he learned of Cipangu and Cathay, Columbus underlined the following words:

pears, precious stones, ivory, pepper, nuts nutmeg, cloves and other spices. . . .

Columbus had planned too carefully to be upset with King John's answer. In 1485, he left Portugal and went to Spain to put his plan before King Ferdinand and Queen Isabella. Five years passed and Columbus suffered much waiting, and much laughter from those who thought him mad. Finally, Queen Isabella was convinced. After all, what had Spain to lose if Columbus were wrong? An agreement was signed, the ships were made ready, Columbus and his crew took communion, and a half an hour before sunrise, August 3rd, 1492, Columbus gave the order and the *Nina,* the *Pinta* and the *Santa Maria* set sail toward the west, to find the East. The little fleet had begun the most important voyage of all time.

From the port of Palos in Spain, the fleet made its way to the Canary Islands where much time was wasted repairing the *Pinta*. On September 8th, all was ready again, and they set sail. One of Columbus' great discoveries was the *trade winds*, and he used them well on this first voyage to sail his ships across the Atlantic.

Mariners had discovered that the seas are divided into certain zones in which the winds often blow steadily and in the same general direction. North and south of that imaginary line around the middle of the earth, the equator, lie the zones of the trade winds. North of the equator the winds blow steadily out of the northeast. It was these northeast trades that Columbus used to carry his ships across the Atlantic. Trace the route that Columbus took on a map and you will see how these winds helped him. Check with your science or geography teacher and find out more about the mysterious zones of winds in the ocean of the air.

No one knows for certain what was in the minds of Columbus' sailors. Few ships had ever ventured more than 20 leagues from land. Each day took them farther into the unknown, farther from home in Spain. Columbus joked with the men and reassured them, and each day he told them they

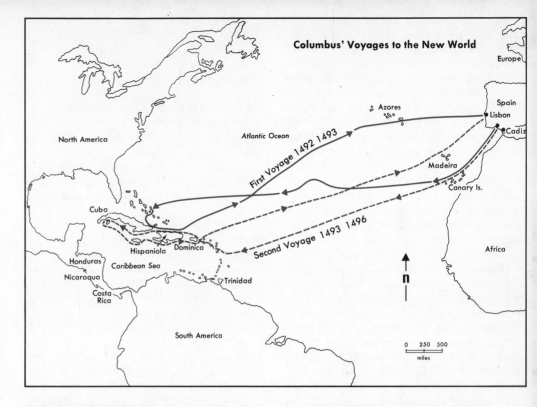

Columbus' Voyages to the New World

Columbus' voyages were a turning point in the story of man. Keeping south as he sailed west keeping north as he sailed back home, Columbus took advantage of the *trade winds* and began a series of voyages that mark the beginnings of a new history of the Americas. This map shows the first two of Columbus' four voyages to America.

had travelled less distance than they really had. He also made much of the various signs they found: reeds, flocks of birds, whales, tropical birds. By the end of September, the crew was restless. Perhaps there was even talk of mutiny behind the captain's

back. Columbus kept on, and on October 12th, the log book read:

. . . they had a rougher sea than they had experienced during the whole voyage. They saw petrels and green seaweed near the ship. Those in the

Pinta saw a reed and a stick, and seaweed, another small stick, which seemed to have been carved with a knife, and small plants which grow on land, and a small plank. The men in the *Nina* saw other signs of land, including a small twig with roses on it. At these signs, all breathed again and were happy. . . And since the caravel *Pinta* was swifter and went ahead of the Admiral, she found land and gave the signals which the Admiral had commanded. This land was first sighted by a sailor called Rodrigo de Triana. . . .

Columbus' crew could just make out the pale shadows of cliffs in the moonlight. What a relief they must have felt, especially Columbus! During the night, the three ships sailed about seeking anchorage. They found the new land to be a small island and called it San Salvador. The Admiral put on his scarlet doublet, and his officers put on their finest clothes. The boats were lowered, and armed with swords, crossbows and lances, the landing party rowed into the shallow beach and waded ashore. Columbus was first, with the royal standard in his hand. Tears in his eyes, he fell to his knees and spoke a prayer.

O Lord, Almighty and Everlasting God, by Thy Holy Word Thou has created the heaven, and the earth, and the sea; blessed and glorified be Thy Name, and praised be Thy Majesty, which hath designed to use us, Thy humble servants, that Thy Holy Name may be known and proclaimed in this second part of earth.

Did Columbus think of himself as a conqueror? What did he think was the first task to be done in the new land?

Columbus was the first to encounter the people of the new land and so that they should be friendly towards him,

I gave to some, red caps and to others glass beads, which they hung round their necks, and many other things of little value. At this they were greatly pleased and became so entirely our friends that it was a wonder to see.

Why did Columbus give gifts to the natives? Why were the Indians impressed with such gifts? Do you think the Great Khan would have been impressed? What sort of gifts do you imagine would have impressed the Khan?

The West Indians came to Columbus in great war canoes and in single smaller canoes, bringing

spun cotton and parrots and spears and other trifles, which it would be tiresome to write down, and they give all for anything that is given them, I was vigilant and endeavoured to find out if they had gold.

After a look around the island and constant exchanges with the natives, Columbus was anxious to move on. What was he looking for? Did he already feel that he had not found Cathay? What would make him think this?

". . . I wish to go and se if I can find the Island of Cipangu." Finding the rich lands of the Orient was never far from his mind. Several excerpts from his diary show Columbus' attitude toward the natives and his purposes.

. . . [about the natives] They should make good servants of quick intelligence, since I see that they very soon repeat all that is said to them: and I believe that they would easily be made Christians, for it seemed to me they had no religion of their own.

I do not see that it is necessary [to build a fort] for these people are very unskilled in the use of arms . . . with 50 men they could be kept in subjection and forced to do whatever may be wished.

I wish to see and discover as much as I can, in order to return to Your Highness in April, if it pleases the Lord. It is true that, if I should find gold or spices in quantity, I shall wait until I have collected as much as I am able. Accordingly I am doing nothing but sailing on until I find them.

I am still determined to proceed to the mainland and to the city of Quinsay in order to give the letters of Your Highness to the Grand Khan, and to request a reply and return with it.

Columbus thought he had reached the "Indies" and called the natives "Indians." How did he describe them? What do you think of such a view?

The boats continued on past island after island, rowing ashore here and there to meet more natives. But he neither entered any of the famed cities of the Orient, nor met the Grand Khan, nor found a wealth of gold or spices. Just before dawn on January 16, the wind freshened and Columbus gave up his search and led his discouraged crew home. For most of the return journey Columbus simply recorded directions and distances. On February 12, the sea rose up and battered the three tired vessels. Columbus wrote:

With my mind in such a whirl, I turned my thoughts to Your Highnesses and endeavoured to find a way by which if I should die and the ship be lost, You might receive news of my successful voyage, so that the victory I had won would not pass into oblivion. I therefore wrote on parchment, briefly as the situation demanded, about how I discovered these lands, as I had promised to do, and about the length of the journey and the course, about the excellence of the country and the customs of its people . . .

To what victory is Columbus referring? Is he trying to tell the King and Queen that he is close to Cathay? Is he exaggerating about his voyage to impress his benefactors?

After sunset, the storm quieted, and on the following day, with his legs almost paralyzed with cold and damp, Columbus saw the rocky coast of an island in the Azores. So ended the most important voyage of discovery in history.

Conclusion

Around 1000 AD Viking sailors saw, and for a short time settled in America. It is not impossible that others made their way across the Atlantic but we have no proof either way. What then makes Columbus' voyage of 1492 "the most important voyage of discovery"? It is what it meant to people, people who were interested in making their fortune, who desired to spread Christianity, who were curious, who wanted power, and later, who sought a new home. In another era, Columbus' discovery could have been forgotten. In his time, this would have been unthinkable. As we shall see, this first voyage was like a falling domino that knocks over an endless line in its wake.

But what of Columbus? He made several more voyages to his Asia. To him his discoveries were a great disappointment. Where were the riches of the Indies? The Great Khan? Cipangu? He died still thinking himself "Viceroy of the Indies." He had found "a new heaven and a new earth."

Columbus had set out to find one thing (the East) and by accident found quite another (America), even though he did not know his error. By accident he became one of history's great men.

Columbus was a dreamer *and* a man of action. He spent ten years studying and convincing others. His courage to test out the unknown began a new era in history. How would you compare Columbus with Neil Armstrong, the first astronaut on the moon?

Chapter 7

John Cabot and the Great Northern Sea

This is how one artist imagined the departure of John Cabot from Bristol. The Bishop would be there to give his blessing, and relatives and onlookers would cheer their encouragement. The sails of the *Mathew* would be made ready and all provisions would be safely on board. The day was May 2 and with fair winds the crew would be back on August 23 with exciting news. The crew of 20 included Bristol seamen, two or three Bristol merchants, one Frenchman and a Genoese barber.

Historians have been lucky with Columbus. There are some things we still wonder about, but for the most part we have letters, documents and descriptions. They tell us who he was, what he did, and why. We were not so lucky with John Cabot.

Cabot was probably born in Genoa about the same time as Columbus. Later he moved to Venice where he became "a very good mariner, of a fine mind, greatly skilled in navigation." He later told a friend that he had been "at Mecca, wither spices are brought by caravans from distant countries," and that he thought these spices must come from Northern Asia. We do not known why he thought this, but when he was in Spain in 1493 and heard of Columbus' triumphs, Cabot decided to try out his idea. Who would be interested? Perhaps England, at the very end of the spice line.

Bristowe on Avon

When Cabot reached England he decided that the seaport of Bristowe, or Bristol as it is spelled now, was the right place to convince people to help him. It was a thriving seaport with rich merchants and beautiful cathe-drals. The docks were busy unloading sherry wine, olive oil, fish, and spices, and loading wool and cloth. Bristol ships and Bristol sailors were famous all over Europe. Cabot learned that Bristol captains had even set out across the Atlantic "in search of the island of Brasylle and the Seven

30

Cities." In 1480, a Master Lloyd "the most knowledgeable seaman in the whole of England" searched the wide Atlantic for months, but did not find "Brasylle."

If good Bristol captains could not find Brasylle, why did this Italian think he could do better? Bristol merchants were willing to give it a try, but they were cautious, so Cabot only got one ship, the *Mathew*. King Henry listened more closely to Cabot than he had to Columbus, whom he had turned down. Spain was building an empire to the south, and England could not afford to be left behind. On March 5th, 1496, King Henry gave Cabot permission:

. . . to sail to all the parts, regions, and coasts of the eastern, western and northern sea . . . to find, discover and investigate whatsoever islands which before this time were unknown to all Christians.

Cabot was to go if he could pay his "own proper costs and charges," and was to be governor of his discoveries. On May 20th, the little *Mathew* sailed down the Avon River from Bristol into the English Channel, to Ireland, and then into the open sea. Cabot kept the North Star to starboard as he headed west. This was much the same method as used by the Vikings, except that Cabot had a compass, a quadrant and a traverse table to help him find his way. Luckily, the seas were smooth and the winds were good, until June 22nd, when a gale rose up. We can imagine the fear and restlessness of the men, 30 days from home over the mighty North Atlantic. Of what happened after we have little proof. An historian of Cabot's time wrote:

In the yere of our Lord 1497, John Cabot, a Venetian, and his sonne Sebastian (with an English fleet out of Bristolle) discovered that land which no man before that time had attempted, on the 24th of June, about five of the clocke early in the morning. This land he called *Prima Vista* that is to say *First Seene*, because I suppose it was that part whereof they had the first sight from sea . . . The soile is barren in some places, and yieldeth little fruit, but is full of white beares, and stagges far greater than ours. It yieldeth plenty of fish, and those very great, as seales, and those we commonly call salmons: there are soles also about a yard in length; but especially there is a great abundance of that kinde of fish which the savages call baccalaos [cod].

Cabot had landed in a distant land. Where was it? What clues are given? Are these enough to tell us an exact location? What had Cabot called the new land? What had he found there that might be of interest to Bristol merchants?

"Prima Vista"

Historians have been guessing ever since where Cabot landed. Cabot himself claimed it was:

. . . the country of the Great Khan . . . the island of the Seven Cities . . .

He was, as an Italian visitor noted, after his return,

. . . called the Great Admiral, and vast honour is paid to him, and he goes dressed in silk, and these English run after him like mad.

Bristol merchants were enthusiastic about "the great abundance of that kind of fish which the savages call baccalaos," but Cabot had his mind on other things. In thinking he had discovered a northern route to the Indies, he had made the same great error as Columbus.

Cabot drew a world map and a globe showing where he had been. These have been lost and the only remaining clue is La Cosa's map of 1500, on which Cabot's discoveries are shown. But the map is not clear. Various historians have suggested that it shows the Strait of Belle Isle, the Gulf of St. Lawrence, the south or east coast of Newfoundland, Labrador, Nova Scotia, or even Greenland. Recent historians have tried to guess by studying old methods of navigation. One suggests that Cabot touched land only a few miles from where the Vikings landed!

The sad story is that we really do not know where Cabot landed. He claimed to have sailed about 900 miles along the coast, taken in baskets of cod, and around July 20th set sail for home. The *Mathew* made it home to Bristol in only fifteen days, a very short time for a sailing vessel, even for today's fast yachts. Cabot wasted no time in travelling to London to inform the King and claim his reward. The King gave £10 "to hym that founde the new Isle." Later he awarded the "well beloved John Cabot of Venice" £20.

The undiscovered country from where no traveller returns

Henry was pleased with Cabot's discoveries, although he had no idea where he had been. Cabot had, however, taken possession for England. In 1498 the King granted Cabot permission to sail to "the land and islands of Prima Vista found by the said John in our name." Cabot

Today the rugged, beautiful coast of Cape Breton, which it is thought John Cabot sighted on his famous voyage, can be toured by the highway which bears the explorer's name— the Cabot Trail.

. . . has his mind set upon even greater things, because he proposes to keep along the coast from the place at which he touched, more and more toward the East (that is toward Asia by sailing westward), until he reaches an island which he calls Cipangu, . . . where he believes all the spices of the world to have their origin, as well as the jewels.

There is no surviving description of Cabot's second voyage either. He set sail, with four or five ships in May of 1498 and disappeared. About fifteen years later an historian wrote:

John Cabot set out this same year (1498) and sailed first to Ireland. Then he set sail towards the west. He is believed to have found the new lands nowhere but on the very bottom of the ocean, to which he is thought to have descended with his boat . . . since after that voyage he was never seen again anywhere.

What had happened to John Cabot? Did he reach the New World on his second voyage? Perhaps his little ships were swamped in a storm or run aground on rocks. Of the man who first set foot in Canada and who laid

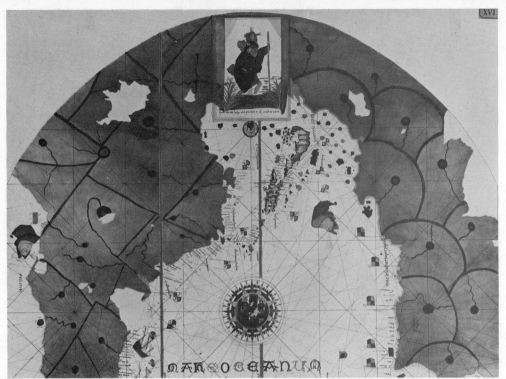

Juan de La Cosa was a map maker who accompanied Columbus on his second voyage in 1493-4. In 1500 he drew this map of America which has confused scholars ever since it was found in 1833. It has been turned upside down, stretched and twisted, but still remains confusing. The Spanish Islands are shown in the centre and that is natural, since La Cosa visited many of them. But to the right of the blowing man is the great mystery—a long coast with English flags! Did La Cosa know of Cabot's discoveries? What does this coast represent? Who gave it the names? Was La Cosa guessing, or did he know something that we do not? Finally, is the map a forgery? No one knows for sure.

claim to the New World for England, history is silent.

The Portuguese in the Northern Sea

It has been said that:

America was discovered by accident, not wanted when found and early explorations were directed to finding a way through or around it.

How true was this of Columbus and Cabot? It is certainly hard to believe that no one wanted the land that is today one of the richest continents in the world, but after Cabot's tragedy men were not eager to sail the Atlantic. Besides, who was interested in rocks, icebergs and fish? Spanish galleons brought back gold and pearls from the south. Portuguese caravels rounded Africa and brought back spices from India. Who would be interested in the northern sea? If you were a European and read or heard Cabot's report why might you be interested?

Joäo Fernandes, an Azorean farmer, or "lavrador," was one of the first explorers to visit America for its own sake. If he could set up a small colony across the Atlantic before Cabot and the English, the Portuguese would control the fishery. Fernandes made one voyage for Portugal in 1498. On a map drawn in 1530 the following words appeared next to Greenland:

This land was discovered by the English of the town of Bristol, but in it there is nothing of value. And as the one who first gave notice of it was a Labrador of the Azores, they gave it that name.

Who first discovered Greenland? How could it be "re-discovered"? The Portuguese called it Labrador, after Fernandes, but later it was given its old Viking name of Greenland. What part of North America today bears Fernandes, the Labrador's name? Fernandes also visited Newfoundland

This drawing was made of a group of explorers preparing for winter on the shore of Hudson Bay. What are some of the many tasks that had to be done? The Portuguese probably had a similar time in Nova Scotia.

on this voyage, but he never had a chance to settle there, as his right to discover new lands was taken from him and given to another Azorean, Gaspar Corte-Real.

Sometime before 1500 Gaspar arrived in the icy seas off Greenland. It was later written that Gaspar had sailed far north into Davis Strait, where he saw white bears and natives who looked like Laplanders. Another writer thinks that Gaspar landed in Newfoundland and entered the Gulf of St. Lawrence. We do not know for sure what happened on this first voyage.

We have several letters describing what happened on Gaspar's next voyage in 1500, however. Gaspar tried to reach Greenland but was blocked by solid ice. He crossed the entrance to Davis Strait and found "a coast where many large rivers flow into the sea." In "a land that was very cool and with big trees and where wild berries

grow," they landed and captured some natives. In October, two of Gaspar's three ships returned, but the third, with Gaspar aboard, was lost and never heard from again. A year later Gaspar's brother Miguel sailed from Portugal to find him. Miguel, like Gaspar and Cabot, was lost and never heard of again.

Although John Cabot had claimed the "new found land" for England, the Portuguese seemed most interested in it. Fernandes, and the Corte-Reals had visited the coasts of Greenland, Labrador, Newfoundland, and perhaps, Nova Scotia. They sent back the first information about the natives of North America, opened the lost Viking route across the great northern sea, and gave the new land its first place names. After these first voyages the great Grand Banks fishery began to grow, and the fishermen became the first Europeans really interested in the new land. Around this time, fishermen

from the Breton coast in France began to visit the coasts around Newfoundland, as did fishermen from England and Spain.

João Alvares Fagundes

After the loss of the Corte-Reals, even the Portuguese dropped the exploration of North America until 1520 when a ship-owner named Fagundes was granted permission to discover lands between "Corte-Real land" and the Spanish land to the south. In 1520 he visited Newfoundland, Penguin Island, St. Pierre and Miguelon and Sable Island. A year later he returned with Portuguese families in the first attempt to build a colony since the days of the Vikings. Historians guess that the little colony was established in Cape Breton, perhaps in the beautiful harbour at Ingonish.

We can imagine the hardships of these Portuguese trying to live in a strange land. They had to build shelter, perhaps plant a few crops. Perhaps they traded with the Indians. They certainly would have caught fish offshore. In a year or two, however, Fagundes saw that his efforts had failed. Perhaps the Indians turned against them or Breton fishermen may have attacked them. The colonists went home. The history of Canada could have been very different had Fagundes succeeded. The Vikings had failed and now the Portuguese. Who could make this new world their own?

Chapter 8

France in the New World

While Portugal, Spain and England sought out Empires in far-off seas, it was as if France, Europe's giant, was asleep. France was the most populated and wealthiest nation in Europe. Why did no French ships sail out seeking the Orient? It is even more puzzling when you learn that French mariners were among the finest in Europe. Along the English Channel were the beautiful harbour towns of Fécamp, Dieppe, Rouen, and St. Malo. The rich merchants of these towns owned great ships and lent money to Kings. True, hardy French fishermen followed Cabot's path and fished the banks around Newfoundland, but it was not until an Italian, Giovanni Verrazzano, came to Dieppe and convinced the merchants, and the King, that ships sailed out under the French flag to make claims for France in the New World.

Verrazzano was "a valiant gentleman," we are told, who was well educated and of "high birth." He told the King that he "intended to reach the happy shores of Cathay." The year was 1523, thirty-one years after Columbus sailed for Spain. Perhaps the King thought it was high time that France took a piece of the pie. So Verrazzano sailed from Dieppe to the Madeira Islands and then into the open sea. In the first weeks, the winds blew "with sweet and gentle mildness," but later storms blew up.

> With the divine help and merciful assistance of Almighty God and the soundness of our ship, we were delivered.

As soon as Verrazzano sighted land, near Cape Cod, he set about searching for the open sea route to Asia. He first sailed south and then north "near the land which the Britons found." He was a careful captain and spent six months studying the American coast. When he returned he wrote:

> . . . The New World which . . . I have described is connected together, not adjoining Asia or Africa . . .

This was a remarkable discovery when you compare it to what Columbus and Cabot thought they had found. It really was a "New" World. But little interest was shown in this "new" world. To most of the explorers of the day, it was simply in the way, blocking the route to Asia.

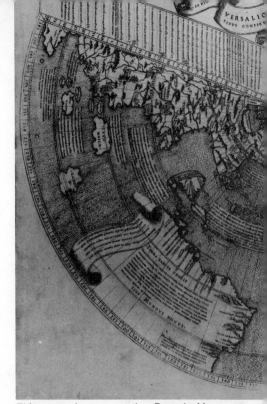

This map, known as the Ruysch Map, was drawn in 1508. It showed between South America (the large land mass to the bottom) and Newfoundland to the north, some Spanish islands, and a wide open sea straight through to the Indies. This is the route that Verrazano believed existed and that he set out to find.

What aroused people's interest was Verrazzano's account that he had seen in the distance from his ship,

> . . . the Oriental Sea between the west and the north. Which is the one, without doubt, which leads to India, China, and Cathay.

Why were people not interested in the "new" lands? Why was Cathay so important to them? What made Verrazzano so sure this was the way to Cathay?

Maps drawn around the time showed this sea and along the coast, was written, "NEW FRANCE, discovered by Verrazzano the Florentine."

In 1528, Verrazzano set out again to find the way to Asia. This time he headed farther south where the poor man was set upon and eaten by a band of ferocious, man-eating Carib Indians. As his friend wrote:

. . . to so miserable an end came this valiant gentleman.

Giovanni had wanted to bring French colonists and Christianity to North America, and to find a passage to Asia. In the latter he was doomed to fail. In the former he played at least a small part.

The New World

In the south, the Spaniards had laid the foundations of New Spain. They settled in the beautiful, warm Caribbean Islands, cruelly set the natives to work, and brought back treasures of pearls, gold and valuable crops. In the north, fishermen visited the coasts around Newfoundland, and men like Verrazzano sought a way around it, but no one thought of settling there. Fagundes had tried, but his attempt ended in disaster. Today's Canada is

Martin Waldseemüller was planning to draw a map of the world according to Ptolemy (see our previous map), but by 1507 news had spread of various discoveries that would forever change Europe's view of the world. We have omitted the right hand section showing Europe and Africa, but the section above shows a revolution from the Ptolemy of 1482. Here we have a whole new continent divided from Asia by a sea. To the right of the map is a portrait of Amerigo Vespuci after whom it is thought Waldseemüller named the new land—America.

so rich that we may find it hard to believe that Europeans did not rush to it immediately, but it is true that the coasts defending our eastern shores are often rugged and forbidding. In those early days there were no docks to moor ships, no hotels to keep visitors warm in the freezing winter. There were no cities of St. John or Halifax or Montreal and no farms in Prince Edward Island. Still, for all they knew, Europeans might find a paradise hidden deep in the dark continent just as the Spaniards did farther south. But was there a way to get inland? What kind of people lived there? The man who came to find out was Jacques Cartier, and he sailed for France.

Jacques Cartier

It was natural for a boy born in St. Malo to look to the sea and to want to grow up to be a mariner. Jacques must have played around the docks and stared up at the tall masts of the great sailing ships of France. His boyhood dream must have come true when he finally got to sea and visted far-off Brazil and Newfoundland. When he returned to France he was presented to the King by the local bishop. "This young man," said the bishop, "has sailed as far as Newfoundland and Brazil, and if the King agreed would command ships to discover new lands in the New World." The King agreed. Perhaps this young man could succeed where Verrazzano had failed.

How do we know about Cartier?

Luckily, we have many more pieces to fit together in the story of Jacques Cartier than we had for John Cabot. Cartier carefully described his voyages, and copies of these descriptions have come down to us. They tell us what Cartier did in the New World, but many of the questions we like to ask about people are still unanswerable. What did Cartier look like? What kind of man was he? We shall have to be satisfied with Cartier's deeds, and guess at the rest.

It is unfortunate for us that there were no cameras in the days of the explorers. Neither are there many portraits of the men themselves for they were seldom gentlemen, or nobles. When later days saw men like Cartier for the heroes they were it was too late to draw their portraits so they often drew what they *imagined* the men looked like. The results, like this portrait of Cartier were often ridiculous. One man has suggested that this portrait looks more like a Russian writer than a French explorer. Whenever we see portraits of historical people, it is necessary to question them as we would any other information. Unfortunately, as far as we know there is no accurate portrait of Jacques Cartier.

First voyage

In 1534, the King of France granted Cartier a sum of money to

equip certain ships which should in company with and under the command of Jacques Cartier make the voyage from this kingdom to New Lands, to discover certain isles and countries where there is said to be found a vast quantity of gold and other rich things.

Questions

1. What reasons did the king give for sending Cartier to sea?
2. What other reasons might he have had?
3. Why would the merchants also want to help him?
4. What was Cartier's position?

The "narrative," as Cartier's description is called, tells how the voyage began:

After the captains, masters and sailors of the vessels had given their oaths, and had sworn to conduct themselves well and loyally in the King's service, under the command of Jacques Cartier, we set forth from the harbour and port of St. Malo with two ships of about sixty tons burden each, manned in all with sixty-one men, on Monday April 20 in the year 1534; and sailing on with fair weather we reached Newfoundland on Sunday May 10, sighting land at Cape Bonavista, Newfoundland. The ice was so bad

This model of *La Grand Hermine* shows a further development of the ship from the days of the Vikings, and from the caravels of the Portuguese. Her masts carried both triangular sails, like the caravels, and square sails, like the Viking ships. She also had high decks and small row-boats for landing. These ships were small compared to today's ocean liners, but they were the finest ships of their day, looked on with pride by their builders and sailors.

along the coast that we found it necessary to enter a harbour called St. Catherine's Harbour, lying about five leagues* south-west of this cape. where we remained for ten days, waiting for good weather, making repairs and fitting up our long boats.

Cartier had made a swift crossing for those days—only twenty days. The winds must have been unusually good. On May 21, the two ships sailed out of the harbour "with a west wind and sailed north as far as the Isle of Birds [Funk Island]."

Here the birds' numbers are so great as to be unbelievable, unless one has seen them. In the air and round about are a hundred times as many more as on the island itself. Some of the birds are as large as geese, being black and white with beaks like a crows.

What a sight Funk Island must have been, teeming with birds. Beothuk Indians used to paddle their canoes to the island to kill the largest of these, the great auk, which sadly is now extinct, as are the Beothuks.

Cartier then sailed northwest about 140 miles to Cape Dégrat (Cape Bauld), a high island cape well known as a landmark to fishermen, and likely the spot visited by Lief Erickson and John Cabot. After a few days spent

*Cartier's leagues are about 2½ miles long. How far would five leagues be?

waiting for favourable winds, they sailed west and then north through the Strait of Belle Isle to the mountainous coast of Labrador. He followed the dangerous coast carefully, never touching bottom. Cartier was a skilled captain. Farther along the coast,

. . . we saw a large ship from La Rochelle that in the night had run past the harbour where she intended to go and fish; and they did not know where they were.

Cartier took the lost fishermen into a harbour he named after himself. We can get an idea of his state of mind from the following description:

. . . the land should not be called the New Land, being nothing but stones and horrible rugged rocks. Along the whole north shore I did not see one cart load of earth . . . there is nothing but moss and short, stunted shrubs.

The narrative describes the people Cartier met as "wild and savage folk." They were clothed in furs and painted and, "have canoes made of birch bark in which they go about, and from which they catch many seals." These may have been Beothuks or Iroquois. The French must have looked just as odd to the Indians as the Indians looked to the French.

We do not know why Cartier did not keep on sailing down the coast, but he changed his course and sailed back to Newfoundland's high mountainous coast which he followed for about eighty miles through fog and heavy weather, before heading back into the Gulf, where he visited Brion Island, a little island "worth more than the whole of Newfoundland," the Magdalen Islands and Prince Edward Island, which he thought was the mainland. Of it he wrote:

All this coast is low and flat but the finest land one can see, and it is full of beautiful trees and meadows . . . but we could find no harbour there . . .

They landed at several places and saw some Indians. The sweet smelling trees, the berries, the wild wheat and the wild life must have been a beautiful sight to Cartier that first summer. Only good harbours were missing.

Next, Cartier crossed to the coast of today's New Brunswick, past Miramichi Bay and into Chaleur Bay, one of the most beautiful areas in the whole Gulf of St. Lawrence, with its rich soil, teeming fisheries and warm climate. Here Cartier

. . . caught sight of two fleets of Indian canoes that were crossing from one side of the bay to the other, which numbered in all some forty or fifty canoes. When the canoes reached shore, they jumped out and landed a large number of Indians, who set up a great clamour and made frequent signs to us to come on shore, holding up to us some furs on sticks.

The Indians seemed friendly, but perhaps Cartier remembered what had happened to Verrazzano. He was greatly outnumbered, and rowed away from them, trying to scare them off. The friendly Indians followed the madly paddling French, but they were finally frightened off by gun fire. Next day, however, the French welcomed the Indians, and

. . . made signs to them that we wished them no harm, and sent two men on shore, to offer them some knives and other iron goods, and a red cap to give to their chief. Seeing this, they sent on shore part of their people with some of their furs; and the two parties traded together. The savages showed a marvellously great pleasure in possessing and obtaining these iron wares, clamouring and going through many ceremonies, and throwing salt water over their heads with their hands. They bartered all they had to such an extent that all went back naked without anything on them; and they made signs to us they would return on the morrow with more furs.

At last there was a happy meeting between the Europeans and the people of North America! Why were the Indians so happy? What did they offer in trade?

Cartier was the first European to visit the picturesque coast of Gaspé. There he met the Iroquois who had come there to fish. Today, little farming and fishing villages dot the coast.

Cartier regretted leaving beautiful Chaleur Bay and its friendly people, but he was certain "that there was no passage through this bay" and so he sailed on, hugging the coast, to the spectacular Gaspé where he anchored on July 16, in "a good and safe harbour."

On account of the continuous bad weather, with over-cast sky and mist, we remained in that harbour and river, without being able to leave until the 25th. During that time there arrived a large number of savages, who had come to the Gaspé to fish for mackerel, of which there is great abundance. They had about forty canoes and numbered some 300 men, women, and children. When they had mixed with us a little on shore, they came freely in their canoes to the sides of our vessels. We gave them knives, glass beads, combs and other trinkets of small value at which they showed many signs of joy, lifting up their hands to heaven and singing and dancing in their canoes.

Cartier went on to describe these people. He was a European and to him they were "the sorriest folk there can be in the world." They grew Indian corn and ate "figs, nuts, peas, apples and other fruits, and beans which they call *sahé*."

On the twenty-fourth the crew erected a cross thirty feet high, with a shield and a sign, reading "Long Live the King of France." The Indians watched the strange visitors kneel down with their hands joined and worship the cross. The Indian chief, Donnacona, had a good idea of what all this meant, and he warned the French in sign language that this was *his* land. But Cartier convinced Donnacona that he really meant to be friends, and he even got the chief to agree to allow his two sons to leave with them for France. Donnacona perhaps knew what a powerful ally the French could be.

Cartier left Gaspé on July 25 and sailed on to Anticosti Island, missing the southern entrance to the great river beyond, either because of fog or a mirage. On July 29 Cartier and some of his men were rowing ashore when his longboat struck a rock "which was immediately cleared by his crew who all jumped overboard to shove her afloat." This gives us a good idea of what Cartier's men thought of him. Anticosti is a cold, forbidding island, but to Cartier it seemed to be a peninsula. He spent a few days trying to discover whether the water to its north led to an open sea or just a bay, and then called his crew together:

. . . we assembled all the captains, pilots, masters and sailors to have their opinion and advice as to what was best to be done. When they had stated one after the other that, considering the heavy east winds that

On his first voyage, by which strait did Cartier enter the Gulf of St. Lawrence? Which major opening to the Atlantic did he miss? Why did he miss the important river opening past Anticosti Island?

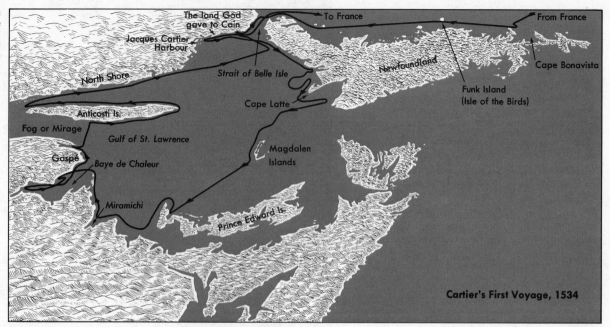

The land God gave to Cain

Jacques Cartier Harbour

North Shore

Strait of Belle Isle

To France

From France

Newfoundland

Cape Bonavista

Funk Island (Isle of the Birds)

Cape Latte

Anticosti Is.

Fog or Mirage

Gulf of St. Lawrence

Magdalen Islands

Gaspé

Baye de Chaleur

Miramichi

Prince Edward Is.

Cartier's First Voyage, 1534

were setting in, and how the tides ran so strong that the vessels only lost way, it was not possible then to go farther; and also that as the storms usually began at that season in Newfoundland . . . it was high time to return home or else remain here for the winter. . . . When these opinions had been heard, we decided by a large majority to return home.

How did Cartier decide what to do? What does this show of his character? What did they decide? Why?

In a gale, Cartier set off for home. Around mid-way to France they suffered "a heavy storm of east winds for three days, but by God's help we suffered it and rode it out. And afterwards we had such favourable weather that we reached the harbour of St. Malo on September 5, 1534." He must have been received with excitement in the little port. He had a coat of arms carved on the entrance to his farm, and his reputation grew. His sailors told of what an excellent mariner their captain was, and what a just man. They would be glad to sail for him again, they said, and soon they were to have their chance.

What had Cartier accomplished? He could tell of rich fisheries, abundant birds for meat, herds of seals and fertile soils. The shores were covered with excellent timber. But the fever of the day was gold, jewels and a route to the Orient. Cartier had made friends with the natives and traded for furs, but there was little interest in fur at the time. From a King's point of view these "savages" were poor indeed. Another voyage was worth a gamble, but not a big one in the King's eyes, for he donated little money for it. Merchants, still hopeful of rich rewards from Asia, offered the rest. He was to set out to "explore beyond Newfoundland to discover far away countries."

Chapter 9

Jacques Cartier and the Great River

In Cartier's time only the small Iroquois village of Stadacona stood on this site, taking advantage of the natural defences.

A captain in the age of discovery had responsibilities before the voyages, as well as during. For his second voyage Cartier was instructed as follows:

. . . by royal command, to conduct, lead and employ three ships equipped and stocked with food for fifteen months, for the completion of the navigation of lands by now already begun, to discover beyond Newfoundland . . . you will buy or charter ships at a reasonable price and as you think good and proper for navigation. For these ships you will engage the number of pilots, masters and mariners as you need.

What responsibilities did Cartier have at home? How long was the voyage to be? What was its purpose?

Second voyage

On May 19, 1535, Cartier set out again, this time with three ships, *La* *Grande Hermine, La Petite Hermine* and *L'Emerillon.* The weather was fine for a few days, but it "turned bad and stormy and continued so for such a long time with continuous headwinds and overcast sky that no ships that have crossed the ocean ever had more of it." After fifty days of battling heavy seas the three ships came together in the fog off Funk Island, where they were warned of land by the screaming of the birds. Cartier wasted no time and headed west into the Gulf.

Among Cartier's crew were Donnacona's two sons who were able to help him find his way, this time past Anticosti, up the river so long "that they had never heard of anyone reaching the head of it." The waters narrowed, and became fresh. Donnacona's sons told marvellous tales of a Kingdom of Saguenay that lay up the swift and dangerous Saguenay River. Cartier anchored there awhile and then sailed on to "where the province and territory of Canada begins." On the high rocks where Quebec City now stands, stood the little Iroquois village of Stadacona. When the villagers saw who it was "they began to welcome them, clamouring and going through many ceremonies." Canoes laden with people came to see the ships and welcome back Donnacona's sons. "The Captain received them all and treated them to what he had to offer." Next day, Donnacona came and in great joy welcomed back his sons and Jacques Cartier.

A pleasant time was being had by all, but Cartier was anxious to move on, especially to the village of Hochelaga, which he was told lay further up the river. Donnacona did everything he could, even performing witchcraft, to prevent Cartier from going to Hochelaga. Eager to follow the great river, Cartier went on anyway, and in *L'Emerillon* passed "as fine a country and as level a region as one could wish," on to Hochelaga which stood where Montreal stands today.

. . . on reaching Hochelaga, there came to meet us more than a thousand persons who gave us as good a welcome as ever a father gave to his son, making great signs of joy; for the men danced in one ring, the women in another and the children also apart by themselves. After this, they brought us quantities of their bread which is made of Indian corn, throwing so much of it into our longboats that it seemed to rain bread.

What kind of reception had the natives given Cartier? Why would they be so happy? How important did Hochelaga seem to be? How has the spot kept on being important even today? How can you explain Donnacona's attempts to keep Cartier at Stadacona?

Hochelaga stood in the middle of the fields which were covered with corn, from which bread was made. It was circular and completely enclosed, except for one gate, by wooden fortifications. Over the gates and at other places platforms had been built from which the Hochelagans could throw rocks and stones for defence against attackers. Within the walls were the longhouses, "each about fifty or more paces in length, and twelve or fifteen in width." Inside were many sleeping rooms and in the middle was a "large space without a floor, where they light their fire and live together in common." They ate corn, beans, peas, cucumbers and

fruits, game and fish and eels. They made their clothing of the fur of wild animals.

Cartier had found and carefully described a very different society from that in Europe.

This whole tribe gives itself to manual labour and to fishing merely to obtain the necessities of life; for they place no value upon the goods of this world . . .

Cartier read the gospel to the sick and then left for Stadacona, much to the disappointment of all. On his return, Cartier sensed that things had changed in Stadacona. Donnacona did not seem happy to see him. But after a while the two were getting along better, and Cartier made ready to endure a Canadian winter, the first to try since Fagundes. The crew built a little fort under the rock of Quebec, brought in firewood, and salted down fish and game. In mid-November, winter set in. The river froze solid. The snow heaped up to four feet. "All our beverages froze in their casks. And on board our ships the decks were covered with four fingers breadth of ice." Then the dreaded disease, scurvy, broke out. The men suffered terribly. By February "out of the 110 men that we were, not ten were well enough to help the others, a thing pitiful to see." Fortunately, Cartier learned from one of the natives, Domagaya, the cure—juices

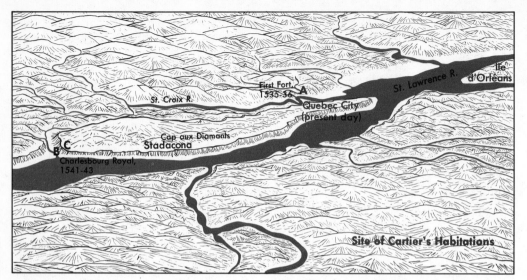

This drawing shows the area which is today occupied by Quebec City. Cartier spent the first winter at the mouth of the Sainte-Croix, near Stadacona (A). Later he moved and built Charlesbourg-Royal at the mouth of the Cap Rouge River. One fort was on the shore (B), and another was on the bluff (C) and was connected by a trail to the lower fort.

from the leaves of a tree which he called *annedda*. It tasted horrible, but miraculously it made the men well (some men said they'd rather die than drink it.) However, twenty-five had died, before the cure was found.

In the spring, Donnacona began telling Cartier great tales about the fabulous Kingdom of the Saguenay. The tales became more fantastic, no doubt, as Cartier's face lit up when he heard the words "gold," "rubies" and so on. If Donnacona was having fun telling these stories to the French, it did not last long. Cartier decided to kidnap the chief and take him to France where he could tell King Francis his stories. Cartier promised to return the chief and the other natives he captured, left more gifts, and set sail for France on May 6, 1536, skillfully making his way down the river to Newfoundland, then across the sea.

Historians describe Cartier's second voyage as very important in the history of exploration. He had accomplished several things. Make a list of these and discuss them. Compare his voyage to that of John Cabot or Giovanni Verrazzano.

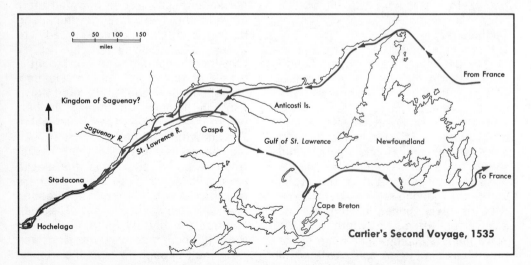

Cartier's second voyage was of tremendous importance to France and to Canada, as he found a gateway into the continent. The Indians had long used the St. Lawrence to reach the Gulf to fish. The French would put it to a different use.

Third voyage

Donnacona charmed the King's ear with his tales of Saguenay. There must be another voyage! This time, however, it would not be a search for Cathay, but for Saguenay, where the French would become great conquerors like the Spaniards to the south. We may wonder why everyone believed the old chief, but the stories of Cortez and Pizarro had seemed no less strange, and they were true.

It was five years before the expedition finally got underway to return "to Saguenay if he can find it . . . to mingle with their people and live among them, the better to do something agreeable to God." Cartier was appointed Captain General and master pilot because of his "good sense, capability, loyalty, prudence, courage, great diligence and good experience." He was granted permission to recruit convicts from the prisons to man his ships. It was hard to convince people to sail to this cold, barren land, unless it was to fish, and return swiftly.

Before the ships set out, King Francis changed his mind and appointed a nobleman, Roberval, over Cartier. Spies spread rumours all over Europe about what King Francis was up to in the New World. Finally Roberval let Cartier go on ahead with his five ships and with colonists and animals on board. Unfortunately, none of the Indian captives were alive to return.

The fleet reached Stadacona in August of 1541. Cartier told the new chief, Agona, that Donnacona had died in France. Things did not seem very friendly. Choosing a spot for settlement at the mouth of a little river, at a place now called Cap Rouge, Cartier named it Charlesbourg Royal. Earth was broken for a garden and the cattle were sent to graze. Meanwhile, the men went about madly collecting what they thought were diamonds and gold. Two ships were sent back to France with the glittering treasures.

In September Cartier set off to look for Saguenay. He passed Hochelaga and portaged one rapid, only to find a worse one, and to hear that more rapids lay up stream. (These are the rapids of the Sault and Lachine today by-passed by the St. Lawrence Seaway.) Cartier decided to return to Charlesbourg Royal. There, relations with the natives had become bad. Agona realized the danger of having the French in his land and felt that sooner or later the Europeans would bring death, whether you were their friend or foe. He must have wondered about the fate of Donnacona in France. We have no records of the remaining history of the little settlement but we can guess that the settlers had a miserable winter. They gave up in June 1542 and headed home, eleven barrels of gold, a basket of precious stones, and seven barrels of silver would hopefully make up for it all.

What a surprise when Cartier entered St. John's, Newfoundland, to find Roberval there! Roberval had three ships and soldiers, masons, priests and doctors. He ordered Cartier to return to Canada, but the weary captain sneaked out of the harbour at night and headed home.

Poor Roberval should have listened to Cartier. His colony became a victim to the cruel winter, disease, and uneasy natives. It looked as if the dream of a New France was lost. There was no Kingdom of Saguenay. There was no route to Cathay. To top it all off, Cartier's diamonds, gold and silver were just worthless metal—"fool's gold."

Conclusion

Most people of the time considered Cartier's voyages to be a waste of money. He, himself, must have been disappointed, although he lived out a happy life with a good reputation. Certainly everyone agreed, then as now, that Cartier was a great seaman, one of the greatest mariners in the whole Age of Discovery. Still, at the time it looked as if the French attempts to settle the northern part of the "New World" were at an end, fated to fail just as the Viking attempts. We know now that it was only a beginning, for Jacques Cartier had discovered the "great river to Canada."

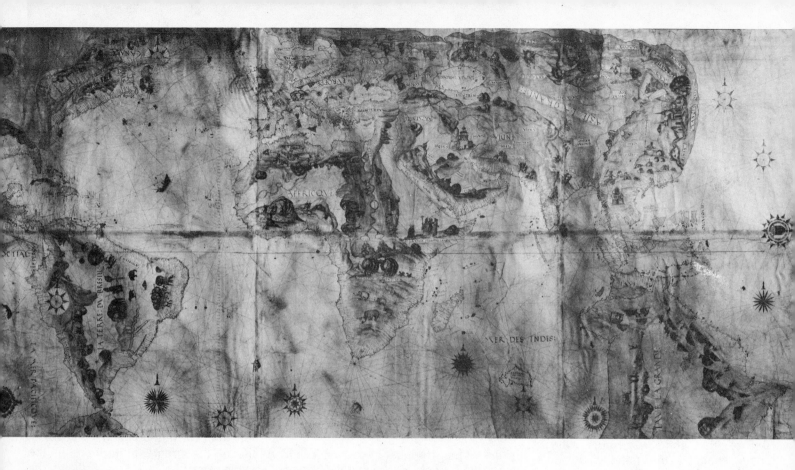

This map of the world was probably published shortly after the discoveries of Jacques Cartier around 1536. Comparing it to Waldseemüller's map of 1507, it shows a great advance in Europe's knowledge of the world. Compare the shapes of Africa and South America with previous maps. Find Mexico and the Caribbean Islands. In the upper right-hand corner, though, is an exciting addition; for the first time the name *Canada* and the Saint Lawrence River called the *Rivière de Canada* appeared. These old maps had many interesting details, often to fill in unknown areas. This map has a small portrait of Cartier in a cloak, which you might find by turning the map upside down and searching the area around the name Canada.

Chapter 10

Discoveries, Past and Future

We began our story with a discussion of what history is about. Now is a good time to go back over that first chapter and use its ideas to summarize what you have learned about the discoveries. What significant facts have you learned? Who were the main characters, and why were they important men?

This is also a good time to stand back and take a look at the whole story. In the beginning, there were no men at all in North America. First to come were the people of Asia, the ancestors of the Indians and Eskimos. They crossed the Bering Strait and slowly made their way to the farthest points of America. Then, thousands of years later, came the Vikings. The Viking chapter in our story is exciting but short for the Vikings did not leave much behind them and they did not make their homes in America. Until recently, their story was almost forgotten but we are now just beginning

Today man's curiosity has led him beyond the oceans, deserts and mountains and into space. What other reasons does he have for going? What will he find there? What a story for students to read 200 years from now!

The heavy waves of the Atlantic Ocean still dash against the rocky shores of Nova Scotia, Cape Breton, and Newfoundland just as they did in the historic days when first visited by the explorers. Rocky coasts and dangerous storms demanded great skill of the navigators. Some, like the Corte Reals and John Cabot, never returned.

to learn more about these early discoveries.

Europeans and the people of North America lived for many centuries without knowing or even guessing that the other existed. As far as we know, the early American people never set out to discover Europe. Even if they had wanted to, they did not have the ships or the instruments to get them across the great North Atlantic Ocean. Europeans stayed home and did not care much what went on

outside their own borders. Then, around 1250, the courageous Marco Polo and his brothers set out on a great adventure to visit the far distant land of Cathay. Soon other adventurers followed the Polo brothers' lead. The mariners of Genoa, Venice, and Southern France and Spain busily sailed back and forth across the Mediterranean Sea. Geographers of Europe began to draw maps showing Denmark, Sweden, Norway, France, Spain, North Africa, Arabia, and even

India and Cathay or China, with its famous cities with strange-sounding names—Cambaluc, Zaytun, Kinsay. But to the west the maps showed nothing. No one expected to find a great new continent between Europe and Asia.

As you have read, there was a great awakening in Europe in the years following the Polos' adventures. Men like Prince Henry, Columbus and Cabot began to wonder what lay across the deep waters to the west.

The miracle of discovery happened because these men and others like them were able, at last, to get the money and the tools to go along with their curiosity. Of course, greed for wealth spurred some of them on. Columbus and Cabot, at long last, had maps, compasses, and instruments to keep them on course and fine little ships to conquer the sea.

Once the voyages of discovery started and the captains returned with stories of new lands and wealth, there was no stopping them. Spain was getting rich on gold from her discoveries in America. England and France set out to establish their claim. To everyone's surprise, what Columbus had discovered was not Asia at all. It was a new continent. The Spanish had every reason to return again to their claim in the south for it was warm and rich in gold and pearls. England and France were disappointed with their new lands to the north, especially the rocky, cold coast of Canada. What use was it?

The story of the English efforts along the coast of North America became the early history of the United States. The story of the French to the north is the early history of Canada. Jacques Cartier was the first man to try and find out about these new lands in the north. Although he failed to find any gold or the so-called, fabulous Kingdom of Saguenay, he left his mark. Why is Jacques Cartier so important in the story of Canada? Cartier had

This drawing of a Beothuk Indian was made long ago, for the story of the Beothuks is one of the saddest in our history. Soon after their first contact with the Europeans, they disappeared forever. The effect of the newcomers on the people of America was often disastrous.

no more idea that a great city like Montreal would one day stand on an island he discovered in the St. Lawrence than we have of what the future holds for our discoveries.

None of these discoverers gave a thought that the land they had found might already be owned by another people. They claimed the lands for their country. They believed that they were bringing the light of day to the "savages." What happened between the discoverers and the people of North America is told in another book

in this series called *The Changing People*.

The story of the French in America is told in the book in this series entitled *New France*.

In the first chapter we suggested that the author chooses his facts to say something. What is the author of *The Discoveries* trying to say by choosing the facts that were used in this book? Is it simply that these were times of great change and of new beginnings to the story that we are still living?

Things to do

1. Write a short summary of what you have learned by using the facts in this book.
2. Choose one of the people we have discussed. Describe what he did and explain why you think he might be called, or might not be called, "a great man."
3. No history book can tell the whole story. Why not? What parts of the story were left out of this one?
4. Build a model kit of one of the ships we discussed and describe how it was important to our story.
5. Ask your school librarian for the titles of some books that might help you to understand more of the story of the discoveries.
6. Compare the exploration of America with the exploration of outer space. How are they the same or different?

I The Expanding World, before Columbus

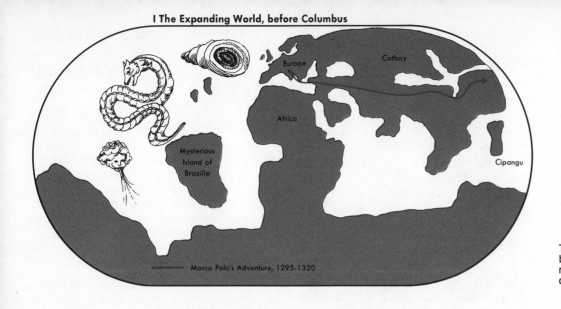

Europe

Cathay

Africa

Mysterious Island of Brazille

Cipangu

————— Marco Polo's Adventure, 1295-1320

This was the world as imagined by Europeans before the discoveries. Compare it with a modern map. Which areas were partly accurate? Which areas were pure guesses?

II The Expanding World, after Columbus and Diaz

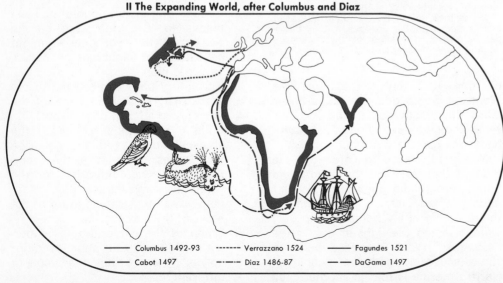

The coloured areas show the fringes of the known world after these early voyages. What has been learned already, since map I?

————— Columbus 1492-93   ------- Verrazzano 1524   ————— Fagundes 1521

– – – Cabot 1497   –·–·– Diaz 1486-87   – – – DaGama 1497

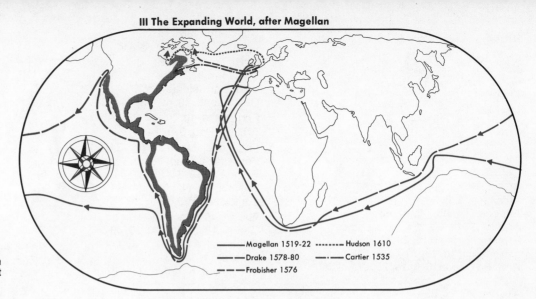

III The Expanding World, after Magellan

———— Magellan 1519-22 ········ Hudson 1610
— — — Drake 1578-80 —·—·— Cartier 1535
— — — Frobisher 1576

What far reaching advances were made in this era? Compare this map to map I. What areas still remain to be explored?

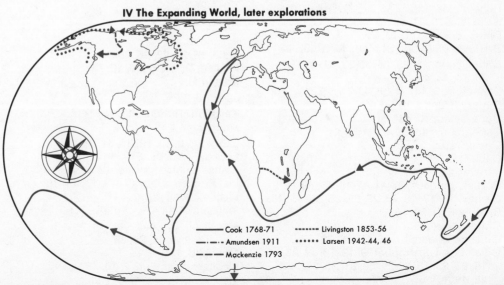

IV The Expanding World, later explorations

———— Cook 1768-71 ········ Livingston 1853-56
—·—·— Amundsen 1911 •••••• Larsen 1942-44, 46
— — — Mackenzie 1793

This map shows the final exciting stage in man's discovery of his world. What new areas have been added? Note that a voyage was finally made across the northwest passage. Man's next great voyages will be into space.

Index

The Collier-Macmillan Canadian History Program

The Collier-Macmillan Canadian History Program

02.970280.1